Critique of the Victim

Daniele Giglioli

Critique of the Victim

Daniele Giglioli
University of Trento
Trento, Italy

Translated by
Sean Mark
Paris, France

ISBN 978-3-031-80131-0   ISBN 978-3-031-80132-7 (eBook)
https://doi.org/10.1007/978-3-031-80132-7

Translation from the Italian language edition: "Critica della vittima" by Daniele Giglioli, © The Author 2014. Published by nottetempo. All Rights Reserved.

Cover credit: © Melisa Hasan

This Palgrave Macmillan imprint is published by the registered company Springer Nature Switzerland AG
The registered company address is: Gewerbestrasse 11, 6330 Cham, Switzerland

If disposing of this product, please recycle the paper.

PREFACE

VICTIMARII. The name given in Ancient Rome to the
subordinate personnel, made up of *popae* and *cultrarii*,
tasked with performing sacrifices. It was the *victimarii*'s task to lead
the victim to the altar and, after receiving the order from the priest,
deliver the blow to the head with the *malleus* (club)
and slit its throat with the *culter* (knife). When the animal was dead,
the *victimarii* would extract its viscera either for divinatory
examination by the haruspices or to prepare the offering
to the gods on the altar (*magmenta*).
The *victimarii* formed a corporation (*Collegium
victimariorum*, Corp. Inscr. Lat., VI, 2191).

—*Treccani Encyclopaedia*

This machine kills fascists

—Woody Guthrie

The victim is the hero of our time. Being a victim grants prestige and
elicits attention, promises and fosters recognition, and is a powerful gener-
ator of identity, rights and self-esteem. Being a victim inoculates from
all criticism and guarantees innocence beyond all reasonable doubt. For
how could a victim be guilty of—indeed accountable for—anything? The
victim didn't act, they were acted upon; they aren't a subject, they're
subjected to. The victim articulates both lack and claim, weakness and

demand, the desire to have and the desire to be. We're not what we do—we're what we've suffered, what we have to lose, what we've been deprived of.

This is a palinode of modernity, with its burdensome injunctions—walk upright, emerge from the state of minority (thus Kant's *What Is Enlightenment?* of 1784).[1] The opposite maxim now pertains: minority, passivity and powerlessness are good; and so much the worse for those who act. The distinction between just and unjust is always ambiguous, but standing with the victim is never wrong. At a time when all identities are in crisis or patently artificial, victimhood entitles us to a supplement of self. Only the victim's hollow form provides a credible—albeit reversed—image of the fullness we aspire to. A 'mythological machine',[2] to borrow Furio Jesi's phrase, pulls from the hollow centre of this lack a ceaseless repertoire of figures able to satisfy the need originating in that very void. The inauspicious has become desirable.

Jesi warns us that those who control a mythological machine pull the levers of power. Victimary ideology is now the first disguise the strong reach for to hide their true motives, like in Phaedrus' fable of the Wolf and the Lamb, where the wolf voices his grievances to get close enough to pounce on the lamb. If only the victim has value, if only the victim *is* a value, casting oneself as such provides a fortress, a strategic position to be occupied at all costs. The victim is responsible for nothing, accountable for nothing, isn't obliged to justify their actions: the dream of every power. By posing as an unchallenged, unconditioned identity, by reducing being to a property no one can contest it, victimhood parodically achieves the impossible promise of proprietary individualism. No wonder wars are fought over it—to establish who's the greater victim, who a victim first, who the longest for. Wars need armies and armies need leaders. Victimhood begets leadership. After all, who speaks for the victim? Who's entitled to? Who represents the victim? Who turns their powerlessness into power? As Gayatri Spivak famously asked, can the subaltern really speak?[3] Is the subaltern who takes the stand to speak for their peers still a subaltern, or have they already crossed over to the other side?

Rather than address these questions right away, let's sit with the disorientation they hopefully bring. The journey from real to imaginary victim is a long and bumpy one, and this sense of disorientation can act as a warning light, if not as guide. It's symptomatic of a wider failure, which works to justify the mythology of victimhood—the disappearance of a credible, positive idea of good. Somewhere along the line, something has gone very wrong. The ancient world, Christianity and modernity all sought to answer the question: What is right? What is needed for a good life? This was an ethical, rather than a moral matter, based on *ratio* and not solely on values. The well-ordered *polis*; the human city as image of the celestial one; *liberté, égalité, fraternité*: these were not only appeals to what ought to be, but created a nexus between ontology and deontology, pointing to a choice—the best available—within the range of the possible. Today, we're stuck instead between the dogma of the lesser evil that informs liberal political thought (democracy, in Winston Churchill's quip, is the worst form of government, except for all the others)[4] and the *mysterium iniquitatis*, the mystery of evil, that elevates to saints or martyrs those who are afflicted, aspire to be or claim to be to legitimise their status.

These are terrible alternatives, accompanied by a host of inevitable affects like resentment, envy and fear. Centred on the repetition of the past, the victimary position precludes any vision of the future. As Christopher Lasch writes in *The Minimal Self*,

> We think of ourselves both as survivors and as victims or potential victims. […] The experience of victimization, which justifies resistance, can also destroy the capacity for resistance by destroying the sense of personal responsibility. This is precisely the deepest injury inflicted by victimization: one finally learns to confront life not as a moral agent but solely as a passive victim, and political protest degenerates into a whine of self-pity.[5]

In his book *Authority*, Richard Sennett builds on this argument:

> The need to legitimate one's beliefs in terms of an injury or suffering to which one has been subjected attaches people more and more to the injuries themselves… 'what I need' defined in terms of 'what I was denied'.[6]

It's disheartening to see our times increasingly epitomised by a pathos-driven formula decoupling feeling from action.

What follows is an attempt to react against this disheartenment. To do so requires a critique of the victim. As all critique presupposes a coefficient of cruelty, it's important to stress that the target of this polemic is of course not actual victims themselves. Rather, it's the transformation of the victimary imaginary into an *instrumentum regni*—a means the powerful exploit to strengthen their power—and the stigma of powerlessness and irresponsibility this places on the dominated. But to deconstruct a mythological machine, we must first disentangle the ambiguous intertwining of falsehood and truth through which it justifies its strength; indeed, imaginary figures are always constructed by combining real-world elements and materials. The world is evidently a great deal more complicated than a Phaedrus fable, and therein lies the work of critique. In its broadest sense, critique is not simply blaming or judging; it's also—indeed, it's primarily, Kant would say—discerning, examining, sifting, delimiting what can and can't be said; it's founding a field, opening a space and finding ground for shared reflection. But critique, Foucault would say glossing Kant, is also a reflection on limits and the possibility of moving beyond them, an attempt to 'separate out, from the contingency that has made us what we are, the possibility of no longer being, doing, or thinking what we are, do, or think'.[7] There can be no critique of the victim from without. Resentment, humiliation, weakness and manipulation are primary data of everyone's experience of the world. This essay is dedicated to all those who don't want to be victims anymore.

Trento, Italy   Daniele Giglioli

NOTES

1. Kant's decree to emerge from the state of minority—which these pages endeavour to follow—may be found in 'What is Enlightenment?', *The Portable Enlightenment Reader*, ed. Isaac Kramnick, New York: Penguin, 1995.
2. See Furio Jesi, *Materiali mitologici*, ed. A. Cavalletti, Turin: Einaudi, 2001, and *Il tempo della festa*, ed. A. Cavalletti, Rome: nottetempo, 2013.
3. See Gayatri Chakravorty Spivak, 'Can the Subaltern Speak?', in *Marxism and the Interpretation of Culture*, ed. C. Nelson and L. Grossberg, Basingstoke: Macmillan, 1988, and *A Critique of Postcolonial Reason: Toward a History of the Vanishing Present*, Cambridge, MA, and London: Harvard University Press, 1999.
4. The ethical-political misery inherent in the apologia of the lesser evil shines throughout Michael Ignatieff's *The Lesser Evil: Political Ethics in an Age of Terror*, Edinburgh: Edinburgh University Press, 2005. For a radical counterargument, see Eyal Weizman, *The Least of All Possible Evils: Humanitarian Violence from Arendt to Gaza*, London: Verso, 2011.

5. Christopher Lasch, *The Minimal Self: Psychic Survival in Troubled Times*, London: Pan Books, 1984, 66, 77. This classic work of 70s sociology provides one of the precocious diagnoses of victimary mythology.
6. Richard Sennett, *Authority*, New York: Alfred A. Knopf, 1980, 150.
7. Michel Foucault, 'What is Enlightenment?' in The Foucault Reader, ed. P. Rabinow, New York: Pantheon Books, 1984, 32–50. Foucault reformulates the work of criticism as an ethos, rather than as specialised technique.

The original version of the book has been revised: Country name in copyright pages has been updated. A correction to this book can be found at https://doi.org/10.1007/978-3-031-80132-7_4

ACKNOWLEDGMENTS

The impetus for this translation, which marks ten years since *Critica della vittima*'s publication, was provided by the 'Essays' residency at the Fondazione Ugo da Como, Lonato del Garda. The translator would like to thank the foundation's staff and the programme director, Giovanni Sciola, for their generosity.

Translations from Italian and French are mine except where otherwise indicated.

CONTENTS

Chapter One

Abstract This chapter charts contemporary manifestations of victim-hood, tracing out a symptomatology of the phenomenon, through examples and analogy. The chapter analyses the victim paradigm under-pinning the state-sanctioned duty of remembrance, and the ways in which it often finds itself opposed to historiography. The chapter discusses the use of victimhood in humanitarianism, a device that governs and spectacularises the production of words, images and emotional reactions in its audience. Broadening its focus, the chapter queries the tendency to portray the twentieth century as an endless, unjustified bloodbath, and omit that it was also, and above all, the century of freedoms, civil and social rights, hope and the narrowing of the gap between the haves and have-nots. The chapter probes the significance of victimhood in a contemporary ethics built on vulnerability, and explores the manner in which leaders present themselves as victims and the necessity of an enemy in populist discourse.

Keywords Victimhood · Remembrance · Humanitarianism · Twentieth century · Ethics · Vulnerability · Populism

First of all, we'll trace a symptomatology of this co-option of victimhood, trying to locate its beginnings, if not its origin, and positing probable

© The Author(s), under exclusive license to Springer Nature Switzerland AG 2025
D. Giglioli, *Critique of the Victim*,
https://doi.org/10.1007/978-3-031-80132-7_1

causes. We'll then move onto critique proper: what victimhood promises and what, especially, it takes away, prevents and renders impossible; why it does so; and what critique might make possible once again. Wherever one looks, there are countless manifestations of this phenomenon—in politics and current affairs, mores and literature, history and philosophy, law and psychology—and it'd be pointless here to pursue completeness. 'People foolishly imagine', Proust writes,

> that the broad generalities of social phenomena afford an excellent opportunity to penetrate further into the human soul; they ought, on the contrary, to realise that it is by plumbing the depths of a single personality that they might have a chance of understanding those phenomena.[1]

Following Proust, we'll discuss a limited number of brief examples, banking on the mutually enlightening value of their unexpected juxtaposition. A process of analogy, rather than exhaustive analysis, will guide the following pages.

Remember Me!

First comes remembrance, our obsession with remembrance. The *duty* of remembrance—a term that in the spirit of our times, as Enzo Traverso has noted, seeks to dethrone history, its twin/antagonist.[2] Unlike history, remembrance is subjective, intimate, lived, non-negotiable, authentic, if not true no matter what. Remembrance is absolute, precisely because it is relative. Inevitably, the relationship it establishes with the past is defined by ownership: *my* past, *our* past. Remembrance is written with personal pronouns and adjectives. At its centre is the witness, and today's witness *par excellence* is the victim—those who bear etched on their body and mind the mark of what they've endured. The suffering subjectivity is the past's true protagonist, which our institutions gladly anoint with state ethics, legally instituting days for public remembrance, like Remembrance Day (November 11) and International Holocaust Remembrance Day (January 27). In Italy alone, February 10 honours the victims of the *foibe* massacres of World War Two; March 21 is the 'Day of Remembrance and Commitment for the Innocent Victims of the Mafia'; and May 9 is the 'Day of Remembrance for the victims of domestic and international terrorism and related massacres', the anniversary of the murder of prime minister Aldo Moro.

Such memorialisation speaks to a sinister disconnect, isolating events from the chain of their occurrence and hypostatising them into values, instead of explaining them as facts. In so doing, it also invalidates the attempt to lend them a cautionary function and prevent what happened from happening again. For it's not those who don't remember, but those who don't *understand* the past who are condemned to repeat it. Remembrance is based on an illegitimate passing of the baton, which seeks to honour those who can no longer speak by filling their silence with the bombast of commemorative rhetoric. Its purpose is for the living, and its true time is the present. What to make, though, of a present that holds up its values only in mourning? That attributes redemptive significance to its dead—as if to say: if we're here today, it's thanks to you?

The prosopopoeia of the victim facilitates a surreptitious substitution. Times and points of view are blurred; the subject of enunciation and the enunciating subject overlap. Like in a figure of speech, the 'we' that pain has cemented and strengthened is and at the same time is not the same that once endured that pain. Whoever speaks as or for a victim always finds themselves speaking in someone else's place. This is obvious when someone speaks on behalf of silent victims, but it's also paradoxically true when victims speak for themselves, since the victim is such precisely because they're forced to remain silent, unheard, deprived of the power of language. Speaking is the first form of agency, while the victim is *in-fans*, speechless. The Nazis knew this well: even if you tell, no one will believe you. But enshrining in law the imperative to listen transplants a judicial logic into the centre of public life (the courtroom, after all, is the only place where the victim's right to be heard is legitimately mandated, even if that speech remains, by definition, partisan), and only further muddies the terrain. Once they've taken the stand, even the most genuine of victims can only be representatives of themselves: we're here for us, and for the you we used to be—you that have claimed the lives of others as your own.

Unjust Mercy

'We're here for you' is also the slogan at the centre of the vast ideological galaxy Philippe Mesnard has termed the 'humanitarian'.[3] Under the guise of a universal morality—one that's unproblematic, and therefore cheap and highly spendable—the humanitarian creed resembles more of a technique, an apparatus regulating words and images, strategically arranged in icons and captions, and the emotional reactions enjoined on its audience:

kitsch aestheticisation, reductive sensationalism and the essentialising of entire populations as victims. Undoubtedly, humanitarian intervention has also been the primary legitimation for almost all recent wars—from Somalia to the former Yugoslavia; Afghanistan to Iraq—superimposing on the gleaming image of the soldier the more reassuring figures of the policeman, the doctor and the sutler.

This isn't the only scandal of humanitarian mercy. Cheap is also the indignation we reflexively feel whenever news of suffering in the world brings to the spotlight personalities like Bernard-Henri Lévy, aka BHL— the most visible and obliging of the *nouveaux philosophes*, who discovered and denounced (in the late 1970s!) the horrors of totalitarianism (Orwell must have been published late in the Livres de Poche, quipped Umberto Eco)[4]—or the many others like him. Simply decrying the manipulative nature of the 'humanitarian' gaze doesn't get us very far: while the ideological framing may be phoney, the framed subject matter is unfortunately usually real. There's no pretend suffering in this world, and this distinction is a vital one.

There is, however, more than one way of showing compassion. What's deleterious here is what this framing does to victims themselves, stigmatising them and giving them an identity that strips them wholly or in part, Mesnard argues, of their biography and their cultural references, or confines them within that biography, while depriving them of subjectivity, and of any rights other than relief, aid or rescue (often with uncertain practical outcomes). The victim's identity is shrunken to what has been done to them. They have tears, not reasons. Their voice, like an animal's, serves only to express pleasure and especially pain, rather than to deliberate in common on what's right and wrong: a prerogative, for Aristotle, that distinguishes the human, endowed with *logos* and society, from other species. The victim's truth is to be found in the gaze of the other—the clement, merciful other. Doctors and reporters without borders, NGOs, celebrities on the rise or on the wane, working ambiguously—at best naïvely—with local potentates or invading armies, are the only parties accredited to speak: 'the legitimate witnesses', notes Didier Fassin, 'who speak in the name of those who have experienced the traumatic events... In the contemporary world, the prolixity of humanitarianism increases in parallel to the silence of the survivor'.[5]

Ostensibly fraternal, the humanitarian creed is a sovereign mode of feeling that subordinates everything it touches; it's on 'the presence of a *police*', rather than 'democratic "conversation"', that 'the regular and everyday operation of [refugee] camps depend'.[6] This is sovereignty without politics, which would instead rely on extending solidarity, rather than to victims, to the exploited, the oppressed or the marginalised with whom we might have interests (a *logos*, a *praxis*) in common—statements that imply a judgement, right or wrong, rather than merely an outpouring of emotion. Designed to elicit these emotions, based on the acritical juxtaposition of feelings and interests, the humanitarian creed keeps the unarmed defenceless (for isn't that what happened in Srebrenica?) and leaves the arsenals of the strong intact, matching outcomes and hidden motives. In Giuseppe Parini's ode 'The Fall' (1785), an elderly man is helped to his feet by a stranger, who suggests he become someone's servant as he has no one to take care of him in his old age. 'You are human, not fair', comes his angry reply to the stranger's pity.

THE GUILTY CENTURY

Humanitarian, and marked by the same flaw of politics, is also the gaze common sense casts on the century from which we've most recently emerged—the twentieth century which saw politics as 'destiny', and is today depicted as a slaughterhouse, indiscriminate butchery, an endless bloodbath. Indeed, it would appear that the twentieth, with its ideologies and conflicts, wasn't the century that narrowed the gap between those who have and have not, those who can and cannot, those who know and do not; it wasn't the century of compulsory education, universal suffrage, votes for women, civil and social rights; of consciousness-raising and speaking out, of choices and dramatic alternatives, of mistakes (for only those who are free are free to make mistakes) and, above all, hope. No, none of this. Rather, it was the century of illusions, mirages and self-delusion. All that was real was the spilled blood, the useless pain of its victims.

Hence the proliferation of Black Books. The Black Book of Communism, of course; but then, in retaliation, of Capitalism. Then, in quick succession: of Religion, the Vatican, Psychoanalysis, drugs, Italian state broadcasting, football, Satanism, the family, high-speed rail. No matter that these things aren't specific to the twentieth century—form has become substance. No longer epic nor tragic, these books are acrimonious laments written to accuse: but you did it too, first, and more, and for worse reasons. The age-old practice of historiographical comparison is back in vogue—comparison, particularly, on moral terms, which historicism and postmodernism, divided in all else, had jointly rejected. Serious scholars naturally keep a disdainful distance from such pursuits, just as they refuse to admit into their ranks the bards of the blood spilled by the defeated—*à la* Giampaolo Pansa, with his splatter historiography that dissolves and fritters away, under the guise of a reconciliatory both-sidesism, the reasons of those who, between 1943 and 1945, fought on opposing sides in our civil war. Though it may preserve academic probity, this gatekeeping doesn't do much to counter a mythopoesis that has to its advantage the voicing of a feeling that's increasingly mainstream. And is this gatekeeping even all that successful? Hasn't the temptation been circulating for some time now—also among academics—to yield to the temptations of a gravedigger's historiography, obsessed with corpses and mangled bodies, mummies and relics, as if there were no life left to be written about?

The same goes for the recent past. In Italy, the 1970s are the years of lead. But what about feminism? Was that leaden too? The kidnapping of Aldo Moro is seen as an epoch-defining watershed, centred on the figure of the blameless victim (albeit a powerful one: as Shakespeare's Hamlet and Manzoni's Adelchis knew, there's no such thing as an innocent path to power). In this telling, it's Moro's unburied corpse that, to this day, is holding Italy back from becoming a normal country—as if Sweden were still living the unending trauma of the murder of Olof Palme. This narrative extends, too, to the aetiological myth of the victimary foundation of our institutions, summarised effectively in Giovanni De Luna's title *The Republic of Pain* (and abetted by the fact that regrettably, as Benedetta Tobagi has pointed out, when it comes to state massacres and political assassinations, victims are often left alone in their demands not for compassion, but truth and justice).[7] That the twentieth century, of which the 1970s ushered in the twilight, was the century that not only practised but also *thematised* violence—humanising and theorising it, reasonably and unreasonably, from Lenin to Gandhi—is an idea that can't be contemplated. For violence, in that case, would no longer be the sole purview of the powerful at the expense of the weak. And isn't that, ultimately, what's difficult to swallow? Inevitably, this narrowing of the conception of violence means today's violence is outsourced, confined to the outskirts of cities and the world. And now it is indeed blind, inhuman and unthinking, deprived of discourse and responsibility and individual and collective actors that deviate from the grim pairing of perpetrator and victim.

IMMUNITY

The perspective is the same if we turn from the public sphere to the private one, from politics to the news cycle. The divide, again, is between victim and perpetrator—the latter essentialised in 'types' that identify them, more than with the acts they perform, with a character, a nature, a destiny, a defining description that becomes a common, even proper noun: the paedophile, the stalker, the homophobe, the racist, the monster, the pack. Instead of an explanation, we're given a nosographic and criminological framework, a marker one either does or doesn't possess, instead of a singular story, an interweaving of causality and chance, of individual events and cultural circumstances. Keep them far away from us—for they are radically different to the rest of us normal citizens, who have no destructive drives in our unconscious and have never once been tempted to subjugate anyone.

In the early twentieth century, Freud had paved the way for an opposite ethics, where there's no ontological distinction between health and mental illness—which doesn't necessarily require organic factors or real-life triggering events, as fantasies can be pathogenic in themselves. The same processes that produce the norm also produce the deviation from it. A framing that means we're all at risk, and therefore called upon to exert control and responsibility. Today's morality, instead, is a morality of monsters, with the victim at its centre and the monster as its only agent. A morality that calls on us to identify not with what we do, but what we don't do (and seek recognition and satisfaction therein), declaring not that we're stronger than those who do wrong, but weaker than them and thus potentially at their mercy. There's something reassuring about this potential being at the mercy of—it works like a vaccine, an immune protocol that strengthens through what in fact divides. How else to make sense of our compulsion to read the entire outside world, both natural and social, through the prism of fear?

It's all too easy, once again, to mock the sensationalism with which the media rehashes—with seasonal variations, but always the same format—moral panics around the serial killer, the sex offender, the paedophile, the gypsy, the Albanian, the Romanian, the Polish plumber, the hit-and-run driver, the Islamist, the illegal immigrant, the prostitute, the junkie, the terrorist, the corrupt cop, bird flu or seasonal flu, the cold snap or heat wave, the dust mite and the Pitbull (but only in the summer of 2004, after which they seem to have stopped biting). Something deeper is at work here, as Joanna Bourke has shown in *Fear: A Cultural History*.[8] One is not always fearful in the same ways and of the same things—being afraid of hell or the plague or the atomic bomb isn't the same as being frightened of Martians or gypsies. And fear, of course, is a primary feeling: you can feign it to others but not to yourself; nor can you think you're afraid without actually being it. But it certainly is possible to deviously induce fear in others, such that it dominates all other affects.

It appears, however, that in the transition from modernity to the contemporary, the frightening and persecutory objects in the social imaginary have drastically increased as their attachment objects have fragmented. An epoch that's frightened of itself continuously inoculates itself with tiny reactants that prefigure a victimisation in effigy, in the hope of averting it in practice. By substituting a 'semantics of life' for a 'semantics of subjectivity',[9] Roberto Esposito has argued, the 'immunitary paradigm' protects the organism to which it inheres: 'it does not do so directly, immediately, or frontally; on the contrary, it subjects the organism to a condition that simultaneously negates or reduces its power to expand', by injecting into the body politic 'a fragment of the same pathogen from which it wants to protect itself, by blocking and contradicting natural development'.[10] The ceding of potency to guarantee survival, implied in the imaginary of the victim, is of a different order to submission to the Leviathan theorised by Hobbes, or Hegel's master–slave dialectic (where the slave is he who fears death), or the renouncing of drives in the name of higher social goals that Freud saw as necessary. In exchange for potency, the position of victim confers a singular form of power; as if, with the crisis in representative democracy, this were the only proper way to divide up and share out power. But power and potency are not the same thing, nor is the 'good life' mere survival. For Christopher Lasch, the attitude of the survivor is a summary, a kind of ethical breviary, of the minimal self, while in Elias Canetti's classic framing, the moment of survival is also the 'moment of power', and powerful is the survivor still standing when the other lies on the ground.[11] That power is gained by usurping its opposite position—that of the stricken, even the fallen; in other words, of the victim—is the paradox we'll now illustrate.

Pity the King

The propensity of leaders to present themselves as victims—the reader will find plenty of examples of this easily enough—is anchored in this paradox. This process is altogether different to the tragic, occasionally comic, dialectic of modern revolutions, where subordinates organise and choose their leaders, and sooner or later those leaders become unassailable autocrats, from Cromwell ending up as Lord Protector to the various leaders of the 1968 groupuscules, via Robespierre and the Bolsheviks. Here, on the contrary, the process is top-down. Though the semantic value of the accusations doesn't change (look what they've done to me, what they've done to us), their pragmatic value is turned upside down, serving now to preserve privilege, be exempted from shared obligations and surrounded by a community of sycophants, whose main commitment, constraint and duty is the preservation of said leadership.

This is not mere deception. Posing as victim, the leader (implicitly or explicitly) offers his followers an affective pact based on identification through the powerful mechanism of resentment. This is the key to all populisms. In many respects, as Ernesto Laclau has argued, populism is a universal phenomenon—a neutral, generic constituent of social interactions. No society, by definition, can satisfy all the needs of its citizens. This gives rise to a number of heterogeneous and asymmetrical demands (for more jobs or more environmental protections; for lower taxes or better welfare), which are at some point placed on the same scale by those mobilising them and thus become political—the expression of a part of society that, despite only being a part, feels legitimised to speak for the whole. The 'people', in this sense, is an empty signifier that may be filled by a variety of meanings, therein lies the effectiveness of the term. The propulsive force of this levelling out of demands hinges on the fact that, should they not be met, it will be *someone*'s fault. For the various parties to forget their original differences and diverse demands, an emotional, and not just rational, bond must be forged between them. It becomes imperative, then, to identify an obstacle, an outsider to be marginalised, an enemy to declare oneself the victim of. Lending the phenomenon a radical ambiguity, this enemy can take on very different guises: aristocrats and capitalists, for example, but also Jews, gypsies, antisocial behaviour, immigrants, scroungers, politicians…

In populism, there's no love without an enemy. And when we identify an enemy, we can't help but see ourselves as their actual or potential victims. This complex knot is difficult to untangle, and the tools of Enlightenment reason are often ineffective, as we may tap into an equivalent, countervailing emotional investment only by deferring to utopia. This can take a doubled form: a liberal utopia, where individual demands are addressed individually; or a socialist one, where humanity is reconciled and the distinction between individual and group no longer has reason to exist. These are remote and unproven scenarios (if they are indeed possible), while resentment is readily available and indisputable.

One advantage of the victimary device is that it requires no mediation. We take its word at face value and need no external verification. When faced with a genuine victim, we know immediately what to feel and think. This is the status that the self-victimising leader (and often the victims' leader) exploits, turning a disadvantage into an advantage by analogical transference. How can you possibly question my pain, he asks, my innocence, my prerogatives? I cannot be challenged or questioned. I am above all criticism, the lord and master of your attention and expression. For you, some utterances are out of bounds—your speech must be favourable to me, or you'll be tarred as executioners. The victim's word, absolute because it's irreproachable, is the most cunning disguise for what Lacan called the master's discourse. Answering only to its own rules and empowered by the victim's right to recompense, such discourse dictates the tone of the interlocutor's reply and the context and terms of the exchange, which it prevents from being altered, for their own (supposed) good.[12] 'The Master', writes Slavoj Zizek glossing Lacan, 'is the one who receives gifts in such a way that his acceptance of a gift is perceived by the subject who provided the gift as its own reward'.[13] Not 'be good, lend me your support', but 'lend me your support and you are good'.

BECAUSE I SAY SO

The co-option of the posture of victim has spread by contagion to fields where we'd imagine different rules should apply. Consider, for example, the increasingly brittle and jumbled field of literature, ravaged by an asphyxiating, blind and self-destructive publishing industry, and drained of the critical spirit that should constitute its lifeblood, if not its guiding principle.

It's worth acknowledging that writers have always played the victim and have often had good reason to—of a literary, more than personal, nature: from Romanticism to the avant-garde, an 'agonal' attitude is a topos of literary history. Even the most unexpected writers have adopted it. Here, for example, is the every-jaunty novelist Alberto Arbasino, in an article entitled 'The Trip to Chiasso', riding high on complaints about the cultural backwardness of his friends, colleagues and fellow citizens:

> Why is it, one wonders, that today we who are not to blame must still feel pained and suffer grievous torment in perpetuity, because a small group of self-taught literati in the 1930s, instead of studying some foreign grammar and making a few trips [across the border] to Chiasso to buy a few important books [...], wasted the best thirty years of human existence whinging in vain and fiddling about inventing the wheel?[14]

Where others pin this backwardness on the long shadow of Fascist censorship, Arbasino is not too tacitly showing off just how advanced he is in comparison to them. The year was 1963. Three years later, the pop group The Rokes sang: 'We see an old world / crumble around us. / But how's that our fault?'.

In recent times, this phenomenon has experienced a quantum leap. Take the case of a gifted writer like Antonio Moresco. Rather than on the undoubted quality of his work, his authorial charisma has been edified on the following paralogism: I, an outcast, still believe in literary greatness, while you powerful people—consummate writers, esteemed critics, cynical and disillusioned publishing executives—no longer do; the fact you won't publish me thus proves I'm great, as it's clear you don't so as not to be proven wrong. Your silence crowns me. I can affirm my own greatness myself. And I'll handpick my fellow travellers, so long as they don't stray so far as to criticise me, which in my terms is tantamount to betrayal.[15] Though not only for this reason, of course, this has landed Moresco deals with all the major Italian publishers, gathering around him a fervent band of admirers, including writers and critics of merit, in the process. That this has occurred in good faith is all the more striking: an exemplary success story against a backdrop of so many other failures destined to oblivion, of which the Internet is both archive and graveyard.

It's no coincidence, in fact, that the victimary attitude has thrived under Web 2.0. Though still under the iron thumb of the big providers, Web 2.0 is also an imaginary paradise of unconnected, unbounded subjectivity, apparently free of all filters.[16] To each user their own access point and the freedom to say absolutely anything they want. But woe to those who challenge us! The rowdiness of mailing-lists, forums and the comments section of blogs and articles provides all the proof we need. Witness the parodic triumph of the critical spirit, nullifying all its virtues and wasting the beneficial, liberating power of negation (critique, for Adorno, introduces negativity into being) in a vicious or idle cycle, usually articulated in four, always identical steps: 1) it's not how you say it is; 2) it's how I say it is; 3) because I say so; 4) and if you disagree, you've got it in for me. The internet has created terrible and wonderful possibilities, and that's precisely why it's full of aspiring oligarchs, sans-culottes who think they're Pythagoras, and Pythagorases who think they're sans-culottes. Real critique is the opposite of fear, ownership, authority and an identity set on always staying the same. Godwin's Law, a humorous paradox, captures the essence of the issue very succinctly: the longer an online debate carries on, the closer the likelihood of a comparison concerning Hitler or the Nazis gets to 1.

COMPETITION

It was only a matter of time before we mentioned Hitler. It's been hard keeping him out of the picture so far, and some may have been surprised by his absence. Hitler and the Holocaust should have pride of place in the phenomenology we're putting together—not the real Hitler and Holocaust, of course, but their obsessive recurrence in the most disparate spheres of contemporary ideology and imagination. And in everyday language too, unfortunately, causing an intolerable trivialisation of a terrible tragedy—where a block of flats is said to have Nazi-like rules and regulations; a poorly managed dog pound is a concentration camp; the social transformation that took Italy from a prevalently agricultural economy to an industrial one is a cultural genocide (responsible for this linguistic shambles is none other than Pier Paolo Pasolini). The Nazi's extermination of the Jews has become the ethical–political paradigm of our times, the source of countless comparisons, parallels, warnings and evocations, both apropos and out of turn.

This is even more paradoxical if we consider that the Holocaust's symbolic efficacy is predicated on precisely the opposite assumption, namely the primacy argument: the most heinous crime, the greatest suffering, the evillest of all evils, with the most victimlike of victims. Seventy years after the events, and with the dying out of those with direct memory of them, this has resulted in turning something no one could ever wish to experience, even in their wildest dreams, into a perverse unconscious fantasy. 'I envy you for Auschwitz', Albert Camus is alleged to have said to Elie Wiesel. This (hopefully apocryphal) story provides a fittingly awful example of the sinister phenomenon Jean-Michel Chaumont has termed 'the competition of victims', the contested primacy of suffering, in other words, the macabre quarrelling of the afflicted.[17] Our genocide was worse than yours; ours is the only true genocide and you have no right to compare yours to ours; ours began earlier; ours lasted longer; you aren't allowed to talk about yours because you haven't yet condemned ours enough; ours was carried out with gas; ours with machetes; ours for ideological reasons; ours for economic exploitation. This also explains the paranoid delusion of Holocaust denialists, who self-victimise by excluding themselves from one of the few assumptions shared by the entire human race, confining themselves in a ghetto of universal execration. Or the astonishing emergence of impostors like the Swiss Binjamin Wilkomirski or the Spaniard Enric Marco,[18] who pretended they'd been deported to Auschwitz when they hadn't. This is evidence not of an ingenious grift, surely, but of something infinitely more painful, the telltale sign of a far more radical lack. These cases bear witness too, but of what? We'll come back to that.

For now, let's put together an essential lexicon of the phenomenon. The key terms here are: lack (mentioned above), primacy, inheritance and impunity. What's lacking, first of all, is the ability to come up with ethical directions and political acts appropriate to the present without pointing continuously to a past that instead of becoming historical is transformed into founding legend, exemplary anecdote or edifying parable. This is the case both for those who hold their own suffering to be unique, and for those who forge from the terrible vividness of other people's catastrophes an affective interpretative scheme through which to understand and communicate their own suffering, with a conflation that only ends up betraying everyone's truth. In the latter case, the right to exist I can't give myself is generated where that same right was taken away from others: their disappearance fills my void.

Primacy, because the need to excel at something is irrepressible. (Misogynists, Virginia Woolf notes, are concerned not so much with the inferiority of women, but with their own superiority).[19] Irrepressible, sure, but also incompatible with a universalistic *bienséance* that's hard to contradict (at least publicly) today, which doesn't allow for cultures or minds to be naturally superior. Nietzsche's 'blond beast', the aristocrat asserting the right to rule, is no longer welcome in polite society. Hence the emergence of this morbid form—an aristocracy of pain, a meritocracy of misfortune, accompanied by the secret (and sometimes not so secret) belief that if they hate us, it's because we're better than them. Hate, not love, is the proof, tuned up to its sharpest chord—envy. The nefarious consequence is that we're only able to love ourselves through the good graces of others' aversion.

Inheritance, because the potential to elicit guilt inherent in the victimary position, actually increases with the disappearance of those who may lay legitimate claim to it. It's usually the descendants of the dead and the survivors who demand a recognition their ancestors never dreamed of asking for. Such recognition is pursued through a logically impossible but rhetorically effective performance. For how can one inherit pain? It's natural for the children of the afflicted to suffer, and reflexively their grandchildren.[20] But after that? And out of devotion to what duty? The absurdity becomes apparent if we flip the perspective: who, of sound mind and upright heart, would call for their descendants to continue to suffer for them? This is tragedy by proxy, a contracting out of resentment. Per its etymology (from the Latin *sentire*), this resentment reveals a spasmodic attempt to feel again what it's no longer possible to feel. It speaks instead to a catastrophic flaw in feeling. For all its ostensible advantages, inheriting an unlived trauma is an indicator of atrophy rather than wealth of feeling. A sad fate to have to usurp from the dead, the surplus of vitality we lack.

And finally, impunity—certainly a pragmatic advantage, albeit a double-edged one. In essence, the heir of the victim demands the same certificate of irreproachability rightfully issued to the person who suffered the harm. But not only are real victims irreproachable only in relation to what they've suffered—such that this safe-conduct doesn't cover their past and future actions—those who are victims only by bloodline are even less entitled to it. This may seem obvious, but isn't. Many international conflicts of the last thirty years can be viewed through this lens (from the Arab–Israeli conflict to the former Yugoslavia, to the Bush administration's disastrous war on terror), with all actors frenziedly seeking a surplus of good conscience in the name of past victims that will exempt them from paying the price for creating future victims—those still avoidable, towards whom the present bears concrete responsibility.

Lack, primacy, inheritance and impunity are the four pillars of the competition of victimhood. It's easy enough to poke holes in all four—the controversy they elicit stems from their obvious fallacy. But each competing victim may point to the other's flaws; exposing the faults of others offers relief from the awareness of one's own. But this is a poisoned chalice, deadlier than the discomfort it seeks to cure. One doesn't become truthful by proving the other person is lying; nor may one anoint oneself as truthful. We see evidence of this in the anguish we feel about not being believed, and the perverse way it's projected onto others (for psychoanalysis, the perverse subject projects their own lack, mutilations and splitting onto others). The attempt to be recognised as first and greatest (if not the only) victim by those with evident doubts about what positive qualities they possess leads necessarily to failure, to the spiteful cycles of the compulsion to repeat—that is, to the death drive.

Vulnerable

Let's pause this brief overview of contemporary victimhood. Many other examples could be added, like the 'recent' discovery of the existence of workplace harassment (as if Fiat workers unionised with the Fiom metalworkers' union in post-war Italy weren't sent to 'isolation wards'), but the overall picture should be clear by now. The mythological machine of victimhood is based on a general proposition, an implicit (and, if it remains unthought, irresponsible) theory of the human, which goes like this: Human is what can be harmed, is what's defined by this susceptibility. Humanity, in this view, is characterised not by the possible uses it can make of its constitutive incompleteness, but by its original lack. Seeing no potency in itself, this mortal race can be protected only through the acquisition of power (fleetingly and while it lasts, hence our obsession with the past and terror of the future).

It's noteworthy, turning to ethics, how perspectives that aspire to see things differently also risk contributing to this outcome—a risk arising, fundamentally, from an unwillingness to criticise the paradigm. We see it, for example, in such statements by Emmanuel Lévinas, perhaps the greatest exponent of contemporary ethics: 'We should think of all the murder there is in death: every death is a murder, is premature, and there is the responsibility of the survivor'.[21] Or when Jacques Derrida, whose work maintains a close dialogue with Lévinas', glosses:

> But to learn to live, to learn it *from oneself and by oneself*, all alone, to teach *oneself* to live ('I would like to learn to live finally'), is that not impossible for a living being? Is it not what logic itself forbids? To live, by

definition, is not something one learns. Not from oneself, it is not learned from life, taught by life. Only from the other and by death. In any case from the other at the edge of life. At the internal border or the external border, it is a heterodidactics between life and death.

And yet nothing is more necessary than this wisdom. It is ethics itself.[22] There's no need to add much here. Our duty to recognise the other is fulfilled only in recording their disappearance. The living other is but a dead person in the waiting room, whose death in effigy I bring forward as I turn to face them. They have something to teach me only because they will one day die—as if they convey nothing essential other than the announcement of my own death through their own. In the other person's heart lurks the same. That's why, for Derrida, strictly speaking, ethics is 'the experience of the impossible', while Lévinas must invoke, as guarantor of the ethical fact, a 'totally Other' that is non-reciprocal because it is immortal, like God.

But isn't this true, too, of René Girard's work? For Girard, everything begins with desire, which is not to be confused with need. Desire is found whenever we want something because someone else also does. Never spontaneous nor innocent, it's mediated, contaminated at its origin by what Girard calls the 'mimetic mechanism'. Rivalry is therefore its natural form of expression. This explains the emergence of conflicts and violence, the constant threat for a human species still on the threshold of animality to implode into self-destruction, were it not for the 'sacrificial crisis': the identification of a scapegoat, in Girard's terms, an innocent victim of a primitive founding murder, able to provide an outlet for the accumulated aggression and anguish inherent in the undifferentiation of desires. Rather than admit the victim is just like us, it's preferable to posit a fictitious difference in the person who's been chosen for lynching precisely because they're exactly like everyone else. Over time, this 'sacrificial crisis' becomes codified as sacrifice: the turning point in the process of hominisation and the first form of social bonding. Every society emerges from it and survives only by its graces. For Girard, this is what all rites and myths refer back to, stories both foundational and deceitful, which work to rationalise the unfoundedness of the sacrificial device by disregarding its cornerstone: the innocence of the victim.

In Girard's work, this cycle, at once salvific and infernal, is countered by the Christian message and its Old Testament prefigurations. Indeed, the Gospel deconstructs this sacrificial logic because it announces the advent of a God who becomes man precisely to take on the role of the innocent victim. Christianity divides human history irreversibly in two: after Christ, no one will be able to claim that the victim is guilty (or, amounting to the same thing: that desire is innocent, unmediated, unmimetic, non-antagonistic). 'Christianity', writes Girard, 'is precisely a way of saying, with maximum emphasis, that the victim is innocent. After all, the victim is the Son of God'.[23] Consequently, for there to be ethics, there *must be* an innocent victim. 'The victimary principle or the defence of victims has become holy: *it is the absolute*. One will never see anyone attacking it. They do not even have to mention it'.[24] That this assumption immediately restarts the perverse cycle of mimetic desire is a problem that doesn't escape Girard:

> One can persecute today only in the name of being against persecution. One can only persecute persecutors. You have to prove that your opponent is a persecutor in order to justify your own desire to persecute.[25]

At the furthest remove from Girard's conception is Giorgio Agamben's *Homo Sacer* series, where the *homo sacer* of ancient Rome—whom Agamben identifies as the archetype of the 'bare life' governed by modern biopolitics—cannot be sacrificed because law has placed him outside of any legal order. And yet, without going over Agamben's cogent arguments, let's recall the three theses presented in the opening book of the series:

1. The original political relation is the ban (the state of exception as zone of indistinction between outside and inside, exclusion and inclusion).
2. The fundamental activity of sovereign power is the production of bare life as originary political element and as threshold of articulation between nature and culture, *zoē* and *bios*.
3. Today it is not the city but rather the camp that is the fundamental biopolitical paradigm of the West.[26]

It necessarily follows that the quintessence of the victim, 'the Muslim, *der Muselmann*', the concentration camp inmate who has reached the limits of exhaustion and indifference to life and death, is also the bearer of 'a silent form of resistance'.[27] A resistance against which the guard's blows appear paradoxically powerless, as a law 'that seeks to transform itself entirely into life finds itself confronted with a life that is absolutely indistinguishable from law, and it is precisely this indiscernibility that threatens the *lex animata* of the camp'.[28] The stricken man who can no longer avoid the blows and no longer wishes to deactivates the law, infecting it with his powerlessness. Since we cannot attribute this 'wish' to someone who has been deprived of all strength, we must see in bare life a *dynamis*, an intrinsic potency revealed only when it's stripped away. It is they, the 'Muslims', those who can no longer bear witness, who are the true witnesses—this is Primo Levi's paradox that Agamben goes on to discuss in *Remnants of Auschwitz.*[29]

Not unlike Agamben, in her books *Precarious Life*, *The Psychic Life of Power* and *Giving an Account of Oneself*, Judith Butler brings into equivalence terms such as relationality, vulnerability and responsibility:

> each of us is constituted politically in part by virtue of the social vulnerability of our bodies—as a site of desire and physical vulnerability, as a site of a publicity at once assertive and exposed. Loss and vulnerability seem to follow from our being socially constituted bodies, attached to others, at risk of losing those attachments, exposed to others, at risk of violence by virtue of that exposure [...] A vulnerability must be perceived and recognized in order to come into play in an ethical encounter.[30]

Here being structurally open to the violence of others isn't an accident but what interpellates and constitutes us as subjects: 'vulnerability qualifies the subject as an exploitable kind of being'.[31] Only by accepting this original datum may we outline the narrow gauge of our capacity to act; otherwise, we run the risk of ethical solipsism and securitarian paranoia. This formulation calls into question the opportuneness of responding to violence with violence, an option under which Butler seems to lump together both revolutionary insurgencies and the policy of the American administration after 9/11:

> That we are impinged upon primarily and against our will is the sign of a vulnerability and a beholdenness that we cannot will away. We can defend against it only by prizing the asociality of the subject over and against a difficult and intractable, even sometimes unbearable relationality. What might it mean to make an ethic from the region of the unwilled? It might mean that one does not foreclose upon that primary exposure to the Other [...] rather, to take the very unbearability of exposure as the sign, the reminder, of a common vulnerability, a common physicality and risk.[32]

Here it's only by learning to inhabit the condition of ontological victim that we may reduce the number of pragmatic victims. First comes the dealing of the blow, then its elaboration, always deferred and structurally incomplete (for to complete it could result in a violent turning of the tables).

To express this in the terms of Axel Honneth, an epigone of the Frankfurt School: there may be recognition if, and only if, there's been a previous, underlying, original misrecognition. To recognise ourselves, in other words, we must first have been disrespected. Honneth claims:

> first, that the essence of everything which, in moral theory, is known as 'human dignity' can only be ascertained indirectly by determining the forms of personal degradation and injury; and second, that it was only such negative experiences of disrespect and insult that turned the normative goal of securing human dignity into a driving force in history [...] If in a concept of the dignity, the complete integrity of man is only to be approximated by determining what forms personal insult and disrespect take, then, conversely, it would hold that the constitution of human integrity is dependent on the experience of intersubjective recognition.[33]

A long time has passed since Adorno, writing in the aftermath of Auschwitz, set philosophy the task of revealing the figures of the false in the light of a truth that is to come:

> The only philosophy which can be responsibly practised in face of despair is the attempt to contemplate all things as they would present themselves from the standpoint of redemption. Knowledge has no light but that shed on the world by redemption: all else is reconstruction, mere technique. Perspectives musty be fashioned that displace and estrange the world, reveal it to be, with its rifts and crevices, as indigent and distorted as it will appear one day in the messianic light.[34]

Today, the opposite has prevailed, and rifts, crevices and traumas are the real, the bedrock. It's down to us to ask what light this sheds on the world.

There's an abyss, of course, separating opportunistic victimhood from these affinities (more than arguments) drawn from the work of Honneth, Butler, Agamben, Girard, Derrida and Lévinas. But it's an abyss that can be crossed—and what brings its two extremes closer is a shared ontology of weakness, bareness and lack, where the human is defined by the inability to act. There's always a void at the heart of an abyss. And it's into this void, which victim mythology aims to fill, that we must now look. What's been emptied out? When did this process begin? We might see this mythology as symptom not of an ontological condition, but of a historical situation. Historical is what once began, the introduction of a discontinuity, the emergence of a 'positivity', in Foucault's terms, that wasn't there before. Fragility and mortality have always existed; victim ideology has not. Let's attempt, then, to piece together those beginnings, if not the origins and causes, and the way this ideology works to put the inherently irrepressible aspects of the human condition to different strategic uses. Let's take a step backwards, then, into a not-too-distant past.

NOTES

1. Marcel Proust, *The Guermantes Way*, trans. C. K. Scott Moncrieff and Terence Kilmartin, revised D. J. Enright, New York: The Modern Library, 1998, 450.
2. On remembrance's domination over history, see Enzo Traverso's *Il passato: istruzioni per l'uso. Storia, memoria, politica*, Verona: Ombre corte, 2006, and *Il secolo armato. Interpretare le violenze del Novecento*, Milan: Feltrinelli, 2012.
3. For the most acute critique of humanitarian ideology, see Philippe Mesnard, *Attualità della vittima. La rappresentazione umanitaria della sofferenza*, Verona: Ombre corte, 2004.
4. Eco's invigorating sarcasm may be found in *Sette anni di desiderio*, Milan: Bompiani, 1980.
5. Didier Fassin, 'The Humanitarian Politics of Testimony: Subjectification through Trauma in the Israeli: Palestinian Conflict', *Cultural Anthropology*, 23.3 (August 2008), 531–558, 539, 537. Fassin and Agier are excellent on the ways in which those providing assistance subtract subjectivity from those they assist.
6. Michel Agier, *On the Margins of the World: The Refugee Experience Today*, trans. David Fernbach, Cambridge, Polity, 2008, p. 63. 'In emergency situations all that matters is victims, and victims, in humanitarian thinking, have no social or political affiliation, and thus no voice' (p. 64).
7. See Giovanni De Luna, *La Repubblica del dolore*, Milan: Feltrinelli, 2011, on the monumentalisation of victims in Italian public life.

8. See Joana Bourke, *Fear: A Cultural History*, London: Virago Press, 2005, on the endemic generalisation of fear.

9. Roberto Esposito, *Living Thought: The Origins and Actuality of Italian Philosophy*, trans. Zakiya Hanafi, Stanford, CA: Stanford University Press, 2012, 262.

10. Roberto Esposito, *Bios: Biopolitics and Philosophy*, trans. Timothy Campbell, Minneapolis, MN: University of Minnesota Press, 2008, 45–46.

11. Elias Canetti, *Crowds and Power*, trans. Carol Stewart, New York: Continuum, 1981, 227–228. 'Simply because he is still there, the survivor feels that he is *better* than they are. He has proved himself, for he is alive. He has proved himself among many others, for the fallen are not alive. The man who achieves this often is a *hero*. He is stronger. There is more life in him. He is the favoured of the gods'.

12. See Jacques Lacan, *The Seminar of Jacques Lacan, Book XVII: The Other Side of Psychoanalysis*, ed. Jacques-Alain Miller, trans. Russell Grigg, New York: W. W. Norton & Company, 2008.

13. Slavoj Zizek, *In Defence of Lost Causes*, London: Verso, 2008, 23.

14. Alberto Arbasino, 'La gita a Chiasso', *Il Giorno*, 23 January 1963. The article was later included in *Gruppo 63: critica e teoria*, ed. Renato Barilli and Angelo Guglielmi, Turin: Testo & Immagine, 2003, 180.

15. See, for example, Antonio Moresco, *Lettere a nessuno*, Turin: Einaudi, 2008.

16. For accounts of the socioeconomic and affective dark sides of Web 2.0, written with first-hand expertise and longstanding critical militancy, see Jaron Lanier, *You Are Not a Gadget: A Manifesto*, London: Penguin, 2011, and Carlo Formenti, *Cybersoviet: Utopie postdemocratiche e nuovi media*, Milan: Raffaello Cortina, 2008. A (tragically) humorous take on the subject can also be found in Giovanni Arduino and Loredana Lipperini, *Morti di fama. Iperconnessi e sradicati tra le maglie del web*, Milan: Corbaccio, 2013.

17. Jean-Michel Chaumont's *La concurrence des victimes. Génocide, identité, reconnaissance*, Paris: La Découverte, 2010, whose title speaks eloquently for itself, is perhaps the work to which this book is most indebted.

18. On imaginary deportations (of Binjamin Wilkomirski, Misha Defonseca, Bernard Holstein among others), see Frida Bertolini, *Contrabbandieri di verità. La Shoah e la sindrome dei falsi ricordi*, Bologna: Clueb, 2010.

19. Virginia Woolf, *A Room of One's Own*. London: Vintage Books, 2001, 28.

20. The matter of the inheritance of traumatic memories is addressed in a deliberately—perhaps excessively— trenchant manner here, borne of a certain impatient nominalism on the author's part. The issue is in fact at the centre of a rich, ongoing debate, which has produced fertile neologisms such as 'post-memory', 'vicarious memory' and 'prosthetic memory'. On the former, coined by Marianne Hirsch, author of many books on the subject, see: Marianne Hirsch, *The Generation of Postmemory: Visual Culture after the Holocaust*, New York: Columbia University Press, 2012. See also: James E. Young, *At Memory's Edge: After-Images of the Holocaust in Contemporary Art and Architecture*, New Haven: Yale University Press, 2000, and Alison Landsberg, *Prosthetic Memory: The Transformation of American Remembrance in the Age of Mass Culture*, New York: Columbia University Press, 2004. Aggravating the matter further is the author's scepticism about any use, beyond the avowedly metaphorical, of the concept of 'collective memory', on which the book by Maurice Halbwachs, *On Collective Memory*, trans. Lewis A. Coser, Chicago: University of Chicago Press, 2020, is excellent.

21. Emmanuel Lévinas, *God, Death, and Time*, trans. Bettina Bergo, Stanford, CA: Stanford University Press, 2000, 72.

22. Jacques Derrida, *Specters of Marx: The State of the Debt, the Work of Mourning and the New International* trans. Peggy Kamuf, with an introduction by Bernd Magnus and Stephen Cullenberg, London and New York: Routledge Classics, 2006, xvii.

23. René Girard, *Evolution and Conversion: Dialogues on the Origins of Culture*, with Pierpaolo Antonello and João Cezar de Castro Rocha, London and New York: Bloomsbury, 2017, 62. The theme of the victim is a fundamental pillar of all of Girard's work, and this book offers both an excellent overview and an insightful introduction to his thought.

24. *Evolution and Conversion*, 184.

25. *Evolution and Conversion*, 184.

26. Giorgio Agamben, *Homo Sacer: Sovereign Power and Bare Life*, trans. Daniel Heller-Roazen, Stanford, CA: Stanford University Press, 1998, 181.
27. *Homo Sacer*, 185.
28. *Homo Sacer*, 185.
29. Giorgio Agamben, *Remnants of Auschwitz: The Witness and the Archive*, trans. Daniel Heller-Roazen, Princeton, NJ: Princeton University Press, 2002.
30. Judith Butler, *Precarious Life: The Powers of Mourning and Wiolence*, London and New York: Verso, 2004, 20, 43.
31. Judith Butler, *The Psychic Life of Power: Theories in Subjection*, Stanford, CA: Stanford University Press, p. 20.
32. Judith Butler, *Giving an Account of Oneself*, New York: Fordham University Press, 2005, 100.
33. Axel Honneth, 'Integrity and Disrespect: Principles of a Conception of Morality Based on the Theory of Recognition', *Political Theory*, Vol. 20, No. 2 (May, 1992), 187–201.
34. Theodor Adorno, *Minima Moralia: Reflections from Damaged Life*, trans. E. F. N. Jephcott, London and New York: Verso, 2020, 263. This quotation comes from the book's conclusive paragraphs.

Chapter Two

Abstract This chapter maps a genealogy of modernity through the victim paradigm, from Rousseau to the War on Terror. In the past, victimhood was one shade among many on a palette dominated by the agency to transform oneself to transform the world, whereas contemporary societies are beset by a preoccupation with identity consolidation. The chapter roots this transition from a heroic to a victimary paradigm in the 1960s, which saw the Holocaust first characterised as a source of pride, and American soldiers in Vietnam portrayed as the war's true victims. Looking at the co-option by capitalism of the demands and watchwords of social movements of the'60 s and'70 s, the chapter explores the unrealisable promise of the capitalist's discourse, and how the dissatisfaction and void it generates prevent the working through of the necessary frustrations of living, instead casting identity as a right and reversing victimhood into a form of prestige.

Keywords Victimhood · Modernity · 1960s · Holocaust · Vietnam · Neoliberalism · fundamentalism

Recourse to victimhood to fill a void of subjectivity is not solely a prerogative of our times. A genealogy of modernity couldn't, for example, omit victimhood's conspicuous importance in the work of one of its founding

D. Giglioli, *Critique of the Victim*,
https://doi.org/10.1007/978-3-031-80132-7_2

fathers, Jean-Jacques Rousseau. From his political works, centred around a thought experiment with a lost original innocence ('a state which no longer exists, which perhaps never did exist, which probably never will exist', he writes of the state of nature),[1] to the mass of his autobiographical writings—the *Confessions, Dialogues* and *Reveries*—Rousseau becomes progressively more afflicted by a persecutory paranoia: put me on trial, convict me, implores the *Dialogues*, and my conviction will be shot through with your guilt. Nor should our genealogy omit the cult of martyrs encouraged by nineteenth-century nationalisms; the miserabilist rhetoric of the labour movement; or the self-victimisation for the pursuit of power that was, alas, already present in the Hitler of *Mein Kampf*.

But victimhood was still but one hue among many, on a palette on which the dominant tones were those of agency, of an impulse to transform the self by transforming the world, of the modernity that Fredric Jameson encourages us to see more than as an epoch, as a trope, a narrative, a temporal gap between subject and object (and Michel Foucault as an ethos, an attitude, a posture)[2]; the very opposite, in any case, of the anxious concerns with identity consolidation that have since beset our societies. Dominant was still the heroic paradigm, as Jean-Marie Apostolidès writes in *Héroïsme et victimisation*, which held out until the 1960s.[3] Then something changed, and the victim paradigm gained the upper hand. Locating its prodromes in the 1960s—a decade we associate with promises and hopes of change, social gains and civil rights—this shift seems paradoxical. How could it have happened?

We Want Everything

The transition from a production society to a consumer society, heralded in the West in the 1960s and continuing to this day, has been given several different names, with varying shades of praise or censure. Neocapitalism, service society, society of spectacle, society of simulacra, postmodernity, hypermodernity—in retrospect, these labels and diagnoses amount to much the same thing. Here we'll privilege the term most congruent with those already used, one which has also enjoyed newfound currency in contemporary thought. What happened, in Lacanian terms, may be described as a transition from the master's discourse to the capitalist's discourse.[4]

Centred on the conflict between the repressing charges and their displacement, the master's discourse is well suited to the proto-capitalist ethic described by Max Weber: abstain, save, accumulate, reinvest, priori- tise the future over the present, draw out your desire as much as possible. The capitalist's discourse, on the other hand, replaces repression with an equally demanding Super-Ego, but one which issues entirely different commands: consume, waste, enjoy yourself; you're entitled to enjoy here and now, everything and all at once, without any hindrance from within and, if possible, from without. The world exists for your pleasure alone; do not submit to the Other's law; trust your imaginary as the truest and fairest thing there is. This is what you're entitled to, and if you're denied it, you're a victim. You—like everyone else, but especially you—are owed access to that ever-lost Thing: fusion with the mother's body; recovery of that original, shattered unity; the end of all toil; the ultimate release of all possible tension.

The capitalist's is an unfulfillable promise, destined to breed perpetual dissatisfaction. In return it offers no possibility of transforming into thought the frustration that, in Freud's terms, helps us accept drive renun- ciation, containment and the discontent of civilisation. No object can fill the void of a subject that has stopped imagining the future and refuses to be held responsible for their past. Like a drug, the mirage of identity tries to remedy this. Identity, here, is understood as ownership, something one has and possesses, ascertainable, inalienable and undivided, undisputed as a natural right, when everything around us increasingly betrays how imaginary, fungible and fictional it is, a performance adopted unthink- ingly because assigned from without, by the whims of commodities, the fluctuations of the market, the omnipotence of finance, the efficiency of the algorithm. Deconstructed by fifty years of postmodern theory, the subject—who acts, mediates, clashes and, in the process, comes into being—is replaced by a simulacrum, all the more evanescent the more it claims to be concrete. The victim posture lends this simulacrum a supple- ment of (apparent) consistency, homoeopathically taking on a passivity that is uncritically reversed into a source of prestige: see, I do have an identity of my own, and now I can prove it, and you all must recognise it. The master's discourse doesn't go away but returns in disguise, tolerant towards the self and intolerant towards others. No longer reflexive or applicable to the self, the 'you' of the 'you must' imperative is extro- verted into a real, external 'you'—a perennial 'you must' or 'you owe me'. Victory is assigned to the most effective identity, the one most able to elicit guilt in others.

Several objections could be raised. For starters, weren't the 1960s also the decade of struggles and demands, of grand designs and, perhaps, foolish utopias (what a conservative liberal like Lacan would call the hysteric's discourse)? It should be clear by now, though, that we're reconstructing a model here, not a general history. This didn't all happen at once, or in the same way. Nor should the advantage of hindsight lead us to flatten all historical difference, so that since this model was victorious, even attempts to resist it were complicit, or of the same ilk. (Berlusconi's mass media 'revolution', as several sharp essays have observed, was a successful'68 of sorts.)[5] Preferable to this flattening out would be a brutally historicist 'woe to the vanquished': in other words, if there were other models, they were emphatically defeated—and, Hegel and Croce would gloss untroubled, so much the worse for them. But discernment is the critic's job. It would be a mistake to conflate the workers' 'we want everything' rallying cry of the Hot Autumn of labour unrest (1969–70)—celebrated by Nanni Balestrini in his novel of the same name[6]—with the 'we want everything' of today's compulsive consumers. But neither are they completely unrelated. The mythology of the victim provides an excellent means of discrimination.

The 1960s and 1970s were a time of avant-gardes, of warnings and harbingers. A genealogical perspective (in Nietzsche's meaning) can reveal how many things, which at first seemed to promise the opposite, became what they are today, without flattening difference or disregarding the intentions of the actors involved. But intentions, of course, shouldn't stand as the ultimate judgement, since involvement doesn't guarantee a more precise or reliable vision of events than an observer's: men make their own history, sure, but don't know or decide how.[7] Only the future can determine what its antecedents were and where they would lead. Let's align some of these, before returning to our current predicament.

SHAME AND PRIDE

June 26, 1967. At a debate in New York organised by *Judaism* magazine, Elie Wiesel, Holocaust survivor and author of *Night*, delivers the following address:

> Why then do we admittedly think of the Holocaust with shame. Why don't we claim it as a glorious chapter in our eternal history? After all, it did change man and his world—well, it did not change man, but it did

change the world. It is still the greatest event in our times. Why then are we ashamed of it? In its power it even influenced language. Negro quarters are called ghettos; Hiroshima is explained by Auschwitz; Vietnam is described in terms which were used one generation ago. Everything today revolves around our Holocaust experience. Why then do we face it with such ambiguity? Perhaps this should be the task of Jewish educators and philosophers: to reopen the event as a source of pride, to take it back into our history.[8]

From shame to pride, the tide had turned. Authors such as Primo Levi and Jean Améry had written searing pages on the guiltless shame of survivors, thematising, analysing, even cursing it, but never reversing it into a source of pride. 'It would be ridiculous enough', Améry had written, 'to boast of something that one did not do but only underwent'.[9] This, however, would become the defeated position, of those facing back to a time when camp survivors were listened to only reluctantly—in Europe and America and even in Israel; when Primo Levi struggled to find a publisher for *If This Is a Man*; when the supervisor of Raul Hilberg, author of the pioneering *The Destruction of the Jews of Europe*, considered it academic suicide to devote oneself to studying such a topic in the United States. In the years between the Eichmann Trial (1961), where for the first time ample space was given to the victims' testimony, and the Six-Day War (1967), an astonishing display of Israel's military power, a tectonic upheaval lifted witnesses out of the shadows and placed them centre stage. No longer merely witnesses, they became judges ('six million accusers',[10] as Gideon Hausner, prosecutor of the Eichmann Trial, wrote in his memoirs), repositories of a message of truth, wisdom and learning. Their testimony was no longer naked, but framed and resignified by an apparatus of pedagogical, penal and military power, which elected it as a permanent mouthpiece. 'In any criminal proceedings', writes Hausner,

> the proof of guilt and the imposition of a penalty, though all-important, are not the exclusive objects. Every trial also has a correctional and educational aspect. It attracts people's attention, tells a story and conveys a moral.[11]

It's beyond our scope here to reconstruct in detail the long, but linear journey that has taken the Holocaust from a source of embarrassment, silence and self-censorship to the object of a veritable civil religion (thanks also to an increase in the attention invested by the media, cinema and television and institutions like museums, schools and universities). Nor will we engage with the interminable debate over the uniqueness and primacy of the Holocaust, its incomparability with other genocides; nor its inevitable public use as interpretive framework and propaganda tool in the conflict in the Middle East (Palestinians as heirs of Hitler; Israelis learning from Hitler, etc.). A huge bibliography exists on the subject.[12] 'There has not been a war in Israel', writes Israeli historian Idith Zertal, 'that has not been perceived, defined, and conceptualized in terms of the Holocaust'.[13] But if invoking Auschwitz initially served an understandable function of national identity building (from helpless victims to never again victims because never again helpless), over time it has ceased to refer to a specific historical event and has become instead a metahistorical permit exempting Israeli leadership from external and internal criticism. The Holocaust, writes Zertal,

> is inserted directly and metaphorically into everyday life in Israel, which is loaded, in this fashion, with meaning beyond itself, as are power and the ideology of power. A quality beyond the secular and the historical has been attributed to this power; the transcendental, inexpressible quality, drawn from the depths of Jewish experience and charged by Jewish victimhood – by absolute Jewish guiltlessness and justice on the one hand and the eternal hostility of a Gentile world on the other – all of which reached their apotheosis in the Holocaust.[14]

Only the victimary position—no longer treated as accident, affliction or external cause (someone doing something to you), but as substance, essence, intrinsic nature—can cement this bond between innocence and power. In secular history, the two terms are mutually exclusive: one doesn't become powerful by innocent means. Powerful, for Shakespeare, are they that have the power to hurt. This explains the need to shift from history to ontology—with talk of being heirs of victims, potential victims, eternal victims and current victims (because they are eternal), who are fully legitimised to act as they wish, without having to answer to anyone but themselves. Nothing is more telling, in this sense, than the (true or apocryphal, in any case revelatory) phrase attributed to Golda Meir: 'We can forgive the Arabs for killing our children. We cannot forgive them for forcing us to kill their children'. Such a statement excludes the possibility that its speaker might one day have to ask for forgiveness, as happens to everyone. They are alone, and untouched by the shared constraints of this world. They refuse to accept their role as an interested party. On top of the right of the mighty they've grafted the right of the weak, striving for a totality without rifts, crevices or internal conflicts. This is identity in the most literal, etymological sense of the word, rather than a historical subject who finds in conflict, first and foremost with the self, an incentive for growth, because conflict is a process that constitutes and structures us, pushing us continuously to rethink our positions.

You Made Me Do It

But let's leave the Middle Eastern question to one side, too complex to be considered in purely ethical and psychological terms. And let's take as given the way in which victimhood has spread, by mimicry, to the other side of the barricades—in the narrative, that is, of Palestinian history in terms of the *Nakba*, the catastrophe: a clear calque of the term *Shoah*. Absent here, too, is any acceptance of responsibility or critique of one's own ruling classes; there is no questioning of one's own positions, of the inadequacies in one's own cultural equipment, of the trail of interests and complicity that has tied the fate of Arab peoples to the fortunes and misfortunes of corrupt post-colonial elites determined to consolidate their influence by offloading all blame onto the enemy without: it'd evidently be immoral to force such a daunting task on those traumatised by catastrophe. (There are, of course, exceptions like Edward Said, but he does so from a minority position, just as in Israel only minorities question the nexus between victimhood and power).

Of greater interest here is how the pattern replicates, with obvious variations, in entirely different contexts. The guiding principle is the repudiation—or the surplus suffering—of a subject that is split, in conflict with themselves, and who, instead of making use of this conflict as a developmental opportunity, disavows it from the domain of their own responsibility. We find a prime example of this in Hollywood's renarrativising of the Vietnam War (more than in history books, memoirs or fiction) by baby boomer directors who had no direct experience of previous conflicts—World Wars I and II, the Korean War—and treated the experience that affected their generation as unique, unheard of, unprecedented.[15]

There are case-by-case distinctions to be made, but let's venture an interpretive summary on the macro level. What unites films by Coppola, Cimino, Stone, De Palma—to name only the best-known directors—is a proposition that may be summed up as follows: we who fought on the wrong side, not the Vietnamese, are the real victims of this war; we who were forced to kill women and children, burn villages, commit horrible atrocities, while our peers in America burned flags and went surfing. Even worse than death was the fate reserved for those who returned—the veterans suffering from post-traumatic stress syndrome, like *Taxi Driver*'s Travis Bickle, who was met with hatred by a youth that in the meanwhile had discovered anti-militarism. We recoil, in these films, from war's error and horror in a way that is visceral, not political: boys lost in the jungle, caught between the fire of an incomprehensible enemy and the orders of superiors who are at best blind and stupid, at worst imperialistic and corrupt. The sorry affair, these films suggest, has nothing to do with them.

Proof of this is the fundamental difference in style between these films and cinematic depictions of World War II (to which we might also add latecomers like *The Green Berets*, set in Vietnam and starring John Wayne). In the latter, world war is presented as heroic, objective epic, following the conventions of the initiation narrative. The former, instead, makes ample use of subjective shots, shoulder-mounted camera, interior monologue or star-lit dialogue between protagonists questioning not whom they should or shouldn't rightfully shoot, but the meaning of their fragile and mysterious existence. This perfect harmony between subject matter and style becomes clearer when, inverting the argument, we consider works that subvert that congruence. Terrence Malick's *The Thin Red Line* is set during World War II, but shot in a style that's exaggeratedly subjective, intimate and pantheistic, to capture the grief inherent in the unbridgeable distance between transient humankind and the eternal splendour of the natural backdrop. But even the first *Rambo* was like this, before the later instalments turned him into a killer with a good conscience.

What did you make us do? You're to blame for so many of our wrongs. We'll never forgive you for what we've done. You never told us how much Monsanto and Rand Corporation were profiting. Victimhood papers over the cracks, neutralises conflict, disavows and displaces it. But the price it pays for this is genuine suffering—the post-traumatic stress of those who, having repudiated from the ego any awareness of psychic contents deemed unbearable, find that such contents return in the real as persecutory hallucinations. Anything to avoid feeling guilty, to dissociate a 'we' from 'you', to avoid and project the sense of responsibility, turning the onus of potency into the relief of weakness. History here is a sacred play of guilty and innocent, and there's no doubt which side decency dictates we stand on. These utopian traces can be glimpsed in parody (which, the Russian formalists remind us, lays processes bare by inverting them) in films like *Forrest Gump*, where the war hero is a simpleton blessed by the gods, or *The Men Who Stare at Goats*, where a Vietnam veteran convinces the Pentagon to fund the First Earth Battalion, a unit of special forces who avert conflicts with a mix of hippy counterculture, Jedi mysticism, LSD and New Age wisdom, and whose motto is: be all you can be. This, it would seem, is the acceptable way to win wars, if not to win tout court.

COMPETENT IN HUMILITY?

A mixture of shame and a fear of winning (with the related, tacit pride in losing) is a common trait of a great deal of the 1960s and 1970s counterculture. *Hasta la victoria?* Onwards to victory? Not necessarily. What happens after that? What do you do the day after the revolution? How do you administer power? Che Guevara would never have become a symbol—his body laid out on the plank like Mantegna's Christ—if he hadn't left Cuba and its regime and headed off to be killed in Bolivia. No victorious Vietcong has enjoyed such a rich iconological afterlife, despite the occasional invocation of Võ Nguyên Giáp and Hồ Chí Minh at rallies and marches. Something similar is at play in the turning into martyrs of rock stars, like Jim Morrison, Janis Joplin and Jimi Hendrix, who died of drug overdoses: scapegoats who suffered for our sins, rather than successful multimillionaires spending their royalties on whatever psychotropic substance they could get their hands on (a rollcall that's continuously updated: Kurt Cobain in the 1990s, Amy Winehouse more recently). Didn't Allen Ginsberg say it in the 1950s?

I saw the best minds of my generation destroyed by madness, starving hysterical naked, dragging themselves through the negro streets at dawn looking for an angry fix.[16]

A whole other book could be devoted to victim narratives about heroin (including the conspiracy theory according to which it was first introduced in Black ghettos, then widened out to all young people, to crush activism). And there was undoubtedly a great deal of sacrificial logic festering in the mind of John Lennon's killer when he committed his crime. It's not difficult, too, to read Pink Floyd's most successful album, *The Wall*, in terms of victimhood—even more keenly in the film version, where the viewer is expected to agonise over Pink's anguish and oppression, for having had a family and an education (a father killed in the war, OK; but add an overprotective mother and strict teachers to the mix, and that's just a step too far), as well as a wife who cheats on him because she's sick of seeing him stoned all the time; a gaggle of eager groupies lusting after him; and, above all, greedy record executives exploiting his talent. There's no worse torture than show business, as singer Edoardo Bennato said.

Granted, these are cheap shots. And we could go even lower, recalling the funeral of Lady Diana, the sad princess who died while speeding at 120 miles per hour in the Alma tunnel in Paris. That the event was watched live on television by two billion people is no joke however, but a very serious matter. Mythologies don't split hairs, that's their strength. But critique can't afford not to. Let's consider, then, some more complex cases (with a mind, too, to unlocking seemingly simpler ones).

Take Pier Paolo Pasolini, for example. Who could deny that it's not only his violent death that contributed decisively to his charisma, but also the ubiquitous victim motifs and Christological identifications scattered throughout his poetic, cinematic and journalistic production?[17] His own mother, Susanna, impersonating Mary before the cross in *The Gospel According to St. Matthew*. The death of Accattone, as Bach's *St. Matthew Passion* plays in the background. Mamma Roma's son tied to the restraint bed in the detention cell, framed to recall Mantegna's *Lamentation of Christ*. The everyman Stracci starving to death in *La ricotta* while playing the good thief on the cross. The know-it-all crow who gets eaten in *The Hawks and the Sparrows*. 'A little too strong your taste for martyrdom, miraculous / sketch of Calvary in which you crown yourself',[18] Franco Fortini wrote of Pasolini in 1956.

It's all already there in his early writings too. In the unpublished prose, for example, of the so-called 'Red notebooks':

Later the express desire to imitate Jesus in his sacrifice to mankind of being condemned and killed even while being totally innocent surfaced explicitly in my fantasies. I saw myself hanging, nailed to the cross. My loins were scantily wrapped by that light rag and a vast crowd was watching me. My public martyrdom ended up becoming a voluptuous image and, little by little, I was nailed with my body completely naked. High above the heads of those present, absorbed in veneration, their eyes fixed on me, I felt I was facing a sky turquoise and immense.[19]

Or in the poems of the *Nightingale of the Catholic Church*:

> Amidst a faint stench of butchery,
> I see an image of my body:
> half-naked, forgotten, near death.
> Such was how I wished to be crucified
> —in a flash of heartrending horror—
> as a child, already my love's automaton.[20]

These energies resurface repeatedly, as in *Poetry in the Form of a Rose*:

> Look, I've been convicted.
> A personal matter, hemlock I must drink alone[21]

(where every syllable, from the opening exclamation, screams it shouldn't be so). Or elsewhere:

> Like a Resistance fighter
> dead before May '45,
> I shall begin to decompose
> ever so slowly
> in the harrowing light of this sea,
> a poet and citizen forgotten[22]

(when it's his brother Guido who died in the Resistance). These lines illustrate Pasolini's mythopoetic genius in projecting his subject matter onto his body—that is, onto his vulnerable, exposed and sacrificeable part (one doesn't sacrifice a soul)—and his body onto his subject matter. This synthesis—of phantasm, metaphor and ideology—offers both an effective scheme of (self-)interpretation for his entire oeuvre, but also acts as a drug inoculating against the 'scandal of self-contradiction',[23] as Pasolini put it in a famous line. Fortini moralistically saw this 'scandal' as the vestiges of an aestheticising affectation; it was, for Alfonso Berardinelli, 'the unshakable pride of the victim'. The victim cannot be contradicted. One cannot be 'competent in humility',[24] to borrow the perceptive oxymoron with which Gianfranco Contini tried to capture Pasolini's contradictory quiddity. In secular history, one is either competent or humble, and it's no accident that the Gospel's message is lodged at the very heart of that disjunction.

The Scandal of History

A) The most adorable people are those who don't know they have rights.

B) People who know they have rights but don't demand them or even give them up are adorable too.

C) Also quite lovable are those people who fight for the rights of others (especially those who don't know that they have them).[25]

Pasolini spoke these words at the 1975 Radical Party conference. The year before, Elsa Morante's novel *History* had been met with a success unprecedented in twentieth-century Italian fiction. Though Pasolini had praised *The World Saved by Kids*, Morante's euphoric sinopia published in 1968, he disliked *History*, judging it a failure, muddled in its ideology and literary technique. As Walter Siti has noted, it's possible that Pasolini made Morante's novel the scapegoat for his own illusions about the proletariat's natural, uncorrupted vitality, illusions he would soon after painfully disavow in his essay 'Abjuration of the *Trilogy of Life*'.[26] For there is, in fact, remarkable coherence in the tone and narrative technique with which Morante illustrates, with unwavering determination, courage and resolve (and a lucidity that always eluded Pasolini), a conception of the world centred on the sanctity of the victim.

History, in Morante's novel, is 'the exploitation of the helpless… by those who have the means to use violence'.[27] 'All History and all the nations of the earth', she writes, 'had agreed on this end: the slaughter of the child Useppe Ramundo'.[28] History, read a caption on the cover of the book's first edition, is 'a scandal that has lasted ten thousand years'. Life's value lies only in those who can be trodden upon. At one point, Useppe, the child in question destined to die of epilepsy (the condition whose aura shines over Dostoevsky's saints and criminals), is told a parable, which sets out the novel's moral. An SS, the story goes, has been sentenced to death. While crossing the courtyard of the prison, on his way to face the firing squad, he sees a flower.

It was a miserable little flower, of four purplish petals and a couple of pale leaves; but in that dawning first light, the SS saw in it, to his amazement, all the beauty and happiness of the universe. And he thought: *If I could go back, and could stop time, I would be willing to spend my whole life adoring that little flower.* Then, as if he had become two persons, he heard inside himself his own voice, but joyful and clear, though distant, coming from some unknown place, shouting at him: *Verily I say unto you: for this last thought you have had on the point of death, you shall be saved from hell!* [...] 'No!' the SS shouted, inside himself, turning back furiously, 'you can't fool me, not again, with those old tricks!' And since his hands were bound, he tore away that little flower with his teeth. Then he dropped it on the ground and trampled it under his feet. And he spat on it.[29]

In *The Drowned and the Saved*, Primo Levi discusses a similar parable, this time told by Dostoevsky:

In *The Brothers Karamazov*, Grushenka tells the fable of the little onion. A vicious old woman dies and goes to hell, but her guardian angel, straining his memory, recalls that she once, only once, gave a beggar the gift of a little onion she had dug up from her garden. He holds the little onion out to her, and the old woman grasps it and is lifted out of the flames of hell. This fable has always struck me as revolting: what human monster did not throughout his life make the gift of a little onion, if not to others, to his children, his wife, his dog?[30]

Finding the parable 'revolting', the contrast between Levi and Morante couldn't be starker.

History caused a lot of controversy. Some, rather spuriously, accused the author of trying to reinstate the traditionalist novel, when even a modicum of attention to its 'posthumous' and self-consciously affected style shows it to be a return, albeit less restrained, to that of *Lies and Sorcery*, her 1948 novel. Others, the self-professed revolutionaries, rejected the novel's content—a fact that will surprise only the naive or hypocritical today, who perhaps exclude artistic production, as petty-bourgeois ideology is rather humiliatingly wont to do, from the realm of serious discourse. Indeed, there was greater respect in rejection: Morante claimed to speak the ultimate truth of being, and on those terms asked to be accepted or spurned.

More interesting and honest is Adriano Sofri's change of heart on the novel. Sofri, the former leader of Lotta Continua (Continuous Struggle), struck up a profound friendship with Morante in the years when he was contemplating abandoning political leadership. As late as 1982, he felt compelled to write to tell her how much he'd actually liked the novel, despite having criticised its message in public. In the letter, he quotes and recants a passage he'd written in 1974, in the aftermath of the Italicus Express massacre[31]:

> How pathetic is this latter-day nostalgia for a history in which the masses succumbed in purity; this false moralism exhorting the masses to stay away from history and power, which are soiled and soiling, and should therefore be left to those who already have them! How ridiculous is the attempt to declare fatal the defeat of the masses in the name of a history that is always the same, always played out on their skin.[32]

Consistently with his change of heart on the novel, in the 1990s Sofri became a leading standard bearer of humanitarianism.

ALICE IN WONDERLAND

Innocence crushed by history—or, amounting to the same thing, saved or preserved by history (meaning both spared, and exalted and glorified by)—is a motif that runs through many of the retrospective accounts by 1970s militants piecing together their and their nation's history. Reading them, one notices how the metaphor of the 'loss of innocence'—often evoked, in the heat of the moment, in relation to the Vietnam War or the Piazza Fontana bombing (as if history and violence began only then)—is superseded by an idea of innocence triumphing even when, and precisely because, it ends in defeat.

This takes two forms. On one side: the cult of the fallen, of *our* fallen, celebrated in anniversaries, every 10 or 20 years, providing a way, too, of cementing the identity of new generations of militants. Indeed, new devotees to the cause have sometimes even used memory to accuse the comrades of the dead of betraying it. 'Out with the new police' was the slogan that rang out in Bologna in 1997, on the twentieth anniversary of the murder by a police officer of Francesco Lorusso, a 25-year-old Lotta Continua militant; the chants, coming from the younger generation of protesters, were contesting the participation in the commemoration of militants from the 1977 Bologna uprising, during which Lorusso was killed, who had since taken on institutional positions. An exemplary case of the transmission of victimary identity transcending the physical bodies of those who, strictly speaking, should be legitimate repositories of said memory. (But, with necessary adjustments and acknowledging the difference in scale, didn't the same logic govern the assassination of

Israeli Prime Minister Yitzhak Rabin, where a young right-wing extremist accused the architect of the Oslo accords with the Palestinians, a man who had ruthlessly fought them all his life, of betraying the ideal of Greater Israel? The real memory of an actually existing warrior is replaced by a hallucinatory fiction based only on indirect experience, therefore all the more susceptible to hyperbole and sacralisation.)

On the other side: the prosopopoeia of innocence as an exemption, a holding back or refusal to participate in the rigged game of history. Consider, for example, this lengthy, but telling passage, in which many motifs of 1960s and 1970s culture and counterculture are repurposed, in reversed but relevant terms, by Franco 'Bifo' Berardi, former member of Potere Operaio (Worker's Power) and leader of the Bolognese 'movement of 77', in a book written ten years after the events and fittingly titled *Dell'innocenza: Interpretazione del 77* (*On Innocence: An Interpretation of '77*). Innocence, writes Bifo:

> reimagines the condition of revolt not as a historical revolt or will to create a just historical world, but as an active shirking, as wisdom. In a sense, innocent thought is the condition of an ability to adapt superior to what the cynics preach. An adaptation able to dismiss historical untruth and thus escape the dimension of historical adaptation, to directly measure the singular experience against a rhythm that isn't that of history, but the flow of time. We replace monotheism's knowing, static god with Hinduism's distracted god, the god who has briefly turned his back to us or fallen asleep, the unknowing god whose moment of distraction begets historical untruth. History, then, looks to us like an accident, the meeting of existential delusion and cosmic play, a dystonia in the flow of time, an excessive thickening in our experience of it. Flows, energies, mental filters, illusions, dreams, imagining worlds: the singular experience, that is existence. Innocence will be able to access the singularity of experience, and the harmony of existential flow and cosmic time.[33]

From this Bifo derives a practical syllogism: 'History kills: let's migrate into (his)stories.'

Many years have passed since'77 and Bifo's evocation of it. Even so, though clearly running counter to the author's intentions, it's hard not to find the experience coveted here as befitting not a revolt, but the daily routine of those who work in finance, invest in equity funds and dark pools—the acephalous swarms of money that aggregate and disperse, with catastrophic effects on people's lives, in the polycentric, timeless and projectless flow of the network, creator and destroyer of worlds, blessed with the innocence of being beyond good and evil. Any Wall Street goon could choose these words as their motto, far removed as they are from both the revolutionary ethos legitimising modern reason and from the morality of Schumpeterian capitalism preaching 'creative destruction' in the name of a responsibility towards the future.

A cruel dialectic, which has seen many of these movements' watchwords implemented, in parodic terms, by their opponents. Here is a brief list, to go with Bifo's advocacy of flow over project. The rejection of work has become the impossibility to find a job. The cult of the free has turned into a society of unpaid internships. Revolt's suspension of historical time (let's shoot the clocks!) has morphed into the ideology of the end of history. The primacy of the body has metastasised into fitness, cosmetic surgery, and the obsession with self-image underlying conditions like anorexia and bulimia. The cult of the inner child, finding the 'child in you' (over the airwaves of Bologna's Radio Alice, named after Lewis Carroll's character; or in Gianni Celati's *Alice disambientata* [*Alice Out of Place*], a book based on his course at Bologna's Drama, Art and Music Studies department between '76 and '77), came to sorry fulfilment when a former adman destined to become prime minister told his salespeople to treat their adult target audience like not especially bright 11 year olds. Dissolution of the subject, rejection of the Cogito, exaltation of the rhizome, joyful suppression of logical connections, wordplay, mass Dadaism, the primacy of emotions: today these constitute the grammar of the imaginary self, interpellated—even performatively created—by advertisers and spin doctors; or of the television audience, which connects nothing and remembers nothing, abandons itself to free affective responses, is unsubstantial, dies and is reborn all the time, at the spur of external events and their changing desires, just as Deleuze and Guattari, the theorists of the *Anti-Oedipus*, described it.

It would, of course, be ahistorical (fancy that!) to hold these phenomena against these movements. But genealogy isn't just about pointing out the bad origins of good things; the reverse can also be true. The capitalist's discourse came also from the mouths of those who fought it—and declaring oneself a victim offers an easy way out.

He Started It

We'd have to wait a few more years before the tendency, described in the previous chapter, to consider the twentieth century (if not, like Morante, the whole of history) indiscriminate carnage would first appear. A good indicator, if not initiator, of this is the so-called *Historikerstreit*, the dispute among German intellectuals that flared up between 1986 and 1987 around the theses of revisionist historian Ernst Nolte. The crux of these theses wasn't to deny Hitler's atrocities but to explain them as a reaction to the atrocities committed by the Bolsheviks, representatives of an 'Asiatic barbarism', which obsessed Hitler and the Nazis. Gas chambers aside, Nolte claimed, the Bolsheviks had already foreshadowed methods and motives later implemented by the Third Reich: concentration camps, torture, mass executions, the will to annihilate one's enemy—class enemy, in one case; racial enemy in the other. With the usual benefit of hindsight (in the meantime, too, Nolte has been largely discredited as a historian for casting doubt, in the 1990s, on the gas chambers), it's clear that Nolte's theories are but a limp rehashing of Carl Schmitt's conception of the twentieth century as a crisis of neutralisation, absolute enmity and permanent civil war. But the thrust of his argument, symptomatic in its blatant fallacy, remains remarkable. Here is its nub:

> Did the National Socialists or Hitler perhaps commit an 'Asiatic' deed merely because they and their ilk considered themselves to be potential victims of an 'Asiatic' deed? Was the Gulag Archipelago not primary to Auschwitz? Was the Bolshevik murder of an entire class not the logical and factual prius of the 'racial murder' of National Socialism?[34]

Let's pass over the racist use of the adjective 'Asiatic'; the nonchalant adoption of an 'as if' logic that borders on the counterfactual (for which the only possible proof would be: had there been no Bolsheviks, then...); and the flattening of historical processes into psychology. The crux of the argument consists in drawing a link between potential victims and factual *prius*: since they considered themselves victims, the Nazis did what they did—a 'since' that crudely conflates causes and motives, post hoc and *propter hoc*. By implication, those who did it first, the Bolsheviks, are the real cause of what was done later. The first has primacy, the origin counts more than the consequence, the cause more powerful than the effect—therefore, the effect is less accountable, less responsible, ultimately the greater victim. Were it not for the tragic subject matter, one could gloss: *He started it, Miss.* But it's impossible not to see the regressive, pre-critical, pre-Aristotelian, even pre-Socratic aspects of such a doctrine of cause: more than historical explanation, it resembles a search for *aitia*, the explanatory factors of archaic foundation myths. Under the semblance of a scientific neutrality that refuses to judge and seeks only to understand, Nolte sets about identifying the guiltiest party—in this case, communism—of which all other, lesser culprits are to various degrees victims.

It's hardly a surprise that these theses, which emerged in the mid-1980s, were met with acclaim in moderate circles, ushering in the tendency of recent decades to discuss twentieth-century history in tones either sorrowful or horrified. Lacking in morality, the capitalist's discourse relies on the same old tools as the master's. Any flaws in the argument may be remedied by victimary ideology, which, when mixed in carefully enough, cleanses everything it touches. Though it didn't for the Nazis, it has worked just fine for many other potential victims lacking in innocence: hence, the proliferation of pre-emptive wars, suspension of checks and balances, and generalised surveillance we've witnessed in recent years. Because victims have the right to defend themselves.

WHY DO THEY HATE US?

This brings us back to the present day. Many other specimens could be added to our discussion. Take, for example, controversies over political correctness. This distinctively American preoccupation has been imported to Europe in a caricatured way, leading to its opposite, political incorrectness, being hailed as the nonconformist position by exponents of a macho and prejudiced culture in places like Italy, where there is very little political correctness or even decency to speak of.

Or take the obsession with literary plagiarism, a scandal bound to resonate in a society beset by a fixation with identity: if they steal mine, it means I have one, and a valuable one at that. Antiquity, modernity and postmodernity each inflected in their own way, and with often inimitable refinement, the fundamental fact that texts dialogue with each other—but this provides little protection today from the abiding, suspicious policing of texts.[35] At stake here is true authenticity, which may be proved, *a contrario*, by the very fact of being plagiarised.

Or the debates about pornography that have divided American feminist theory. On one side are those who, like Andrea Dworkin and Catharine MacKinnon, suggest banning pornography, seeing it as a linguistic act that performatively does what it says—namely, humiliate and subjugate women. On the other are those, like Nadine Strossen or Judith Butler, who dwell instead on the message's 'perlocutionary' function, in the terms of J. L. Austin, the founder of the theory of linguistic acts—the psychological effect, in other words, the message produces on its recipient, which cannot be controlled by the authority of the emitter or the context of emission (as is the case with 'illocutionary' utterances, like 'I baptise you', 'I absolve you', or 'I proclaim you husband and wife').[36] For Dworkin and MacKinnon, women who perform or consume pornography are always victims, because the message's illocutionary force nullifies their agency, regardless of consent or gratification. For Strossen and Butler, on the other hand, establishing (dis)value by the force of law (with its truly illocutionary 'it is forbidden') creates an authoritarian framing in which some women, in the role of mothers or older sisters, arrogate the duty of viewing pornographic material to prevent less enlightened daughters or sisters from doing so—and it's this, if anything, that nullifies agency. Arrogating the role of representatives of alleged victims, the latter position themselves as leaders by confiscating their rights, if only to determine whether they are in the right or wrong. The victim argument always has the pathos of the unimpeachable on its side.

The so-called clash of 'civilisations' or 'cultures', with which the new millennium began in the wake of 9/11, may also be seen as a conflict between unimpeachables. This extraordinary event was steeped, in advance and in retrospect, with victimary motives that it would be wrong to see merely as ideological cover for far more terrestrial interests—the Middle Eastern chessboard, for example, or the control of oil reserves. Not that these tacit interests were immaterial or uninfluential, of course—the Trojan war wasn't just about Helen. But it's also true, to paraphrase Ernst Bloch, that no one gives up their life for the five-year plan. Other impulses lead men and women to take fate into their hands, and whittling them down isn't historical materialism but a crude version of rational choice theory, by which everyone acts only to maximise their own profit. 'Why do they hate us?', George W. Bush's naive, perhaps even sincere question, on the verge of dumping thousands of tonnes of bombs on the people of Central Asia, captured the phenomenon better. Fuelling the victimary device here is the demand to be loved and an inability to accept the possibility of it not being so, which can easily spill over into a will to annihilate. What to do, Slavoj Zizek glosses, when the Other is really other? The answer, it seems, is: hypostatise this difference into 'cultures' (a logical fallacy, which concludes what it sets out to prove), or debase our language and thinking to the point of positing a 'clash' (or meeting, which amounts to the same thing) between 'cultures' or 'civilisations', rather than subjects. For all their showy opposition to one another, well-meaning multiculturalism and aggressive neoconservatism secretly agree, sharing a paradigm and reasoning with the same assumptions. Significantly, they fight over the remains of the victim, like the Greeks and the Trojans over Patroclus' body.

A case in point is the murder of Theo van Gogh, the director of *Submission*, a short film that caused offence among Muslims for projecting verses from the Quran onto the naked bodies of several young women, as a voiceover asks Allah whether the oppression endured by women in Islamic tradition is in accordance with his will. In a thorough and detailed account, Ian Buruma pieces together the circumstances and context of the murder.[37] Mohammed Bouyeri, a young Dutch man of Moroccan origin, ensnared by fundamentalist material he mostly sources online, stabs and shoots van Gogh to death on November 2, 2004, pinning to his chest a letter, full of Quranic rhetoric poorly translated from English into Dutch. Bouyeri doesn't speak Arabic and went to commit the murder by bicycle, just as van Gogh was also on his bicycle. Alongside Theo and Mohammed's story, Buruma writes about Ayaan Hirsi Ali, the Somali-born Dutch politician and scriptwriter of *Submission*, who has become the darling of the neoconservative right since stating that Islam and democracy are incompatible. Another chapter of Buruma's book is devoted to the histrionic populist leader Pim Fortuyn, a man of many contradictions—homosexual and xenophobic, liberal and intolerant—who was also assassinated, in 2002, by an animal rights fanatic. Buruma gathers testimony from family members, politicians and intellectuals—very large are the ranks of former leftists who now curse multiculturalism—and fundamentalist and moderate imams. In the background are four decades of Dutch history, from the first shockwaves to the Calvinist edifice in the 1960s (the Provo movement, anti-colonialism, sexual liberation, drugs), to the utopia of conflict-free coexistence that shrivelled up in the late 1990s. Verily, the capitalist's discourse is in trouble without the master's.

What unites these four characters, who follow the script assigned to them by the 'clash of civilisations' narrative with the efficiency of automatons, is their attitude of aggressive victimhood. Aggressive first and foremost is Theo van Gogh, who seeks inspiration in insult, calls Muslims 'goatfuckers', says Christ is worth no more than a dead fish and insinuates that some Jewish women only find pleasure if they dream of being raped by Dr. Mengele, evidently convinced that freedom primarily means freedom to offend. Aggressive, of course, is his murderer, Mohammed Bouyeri—a typical example of the radicalised loser who casts himself as avenger of a third-hand Islam to mask his self-loathing and contempt for his own failures, and who can only find satisfaction in a sensational and self-destructive act. Aggressive is Pim Fortuyn, a mediocre academic of modest cultural standing turned fear-monger, who, under the cover of his homosexuality, stirs intolerance for immigrants who—it's their culture, everybody knows—would never tolerate homosexuals should they become a majority in the country: a fine problem at least since John Locke's *A Letter Concerning Toleration*, but one that isn't solved by theatrics. Aggressive, too, is Ayaan Hirsi Ali, who lectures on the failure of Islamic enlightenment by comparing it with a European enlightenment she manifestly knows nothing about, uses Joan of Arc-like rhetoric, and is so modest as to compare herself to Spinoza.

Narcissism, resentment, platitudes, truisms: we must respect others, yes, so long as they respect us. Where fanatics and opportunists clamour, the reasonable stutter—and Buruma himself can't suggest a way out of the impasse, not least because all the contenders, even the murderer, have half-truths on their side. Indeed, this case provides an excellent example of truth as a moment of the false. The only other option is to break the bank, refuse to be held to ransom, and critique the very terms of the debate. And that's what remains to be done in the pages that follow.

NOTES

1. Jean-Jacques Rousseau, 'Discourse on the Origin and Foundations of Inequality Among Men or Second Discourse', trans. V. Gourevitch, in *Rousseau: The Discourses and Other Early Political Writings*, ed. V. Gourevitch (Cambridge: Cambridge University Press, 1997), 125.
2. Fredric Jameson, *A Singular Modernity: Essay on the Ontology of the Present*, London: Verso, 2002.
3. Jean-Marie Apostolidès, *Héroïsme et victimisation. Une histoire de la sensibilité*, Paris: Les Editions du Cerf, 2011.

4. The addition of the 'capitalist's discourse' to the theory of the 'four discourses' was formulated by Jacques Lacan in a lecture in Milan in 1972 ('Del discorso psicoanalitico', in *Lacan in Italia. 1953–1978*, ed. G. Contri, Milan: La Salamandra, 1978). Today, it's widely known through the work of Massimo Recalcati, particularly his *L'uomo senza inconscio: Figure della nuova clinica psicoanalitica*, Milan: Raffaello Cortina, 2010.

5. For sophisticated and knowingly one-sided pamphlets—which criticise 'from the left', rather than in the name of eternal Italian moderatism, the limits of ''68' (the quotation marks underline the focus on the iconic afterlife, rather than the actual historical phenomenon)—see: Valerio Magrelli, *Il Sessantotto realizzato da Mediaset*, Turin: Einaudi, 2011, and Mario Perniola, *Berlusconi o il'68 realizzato*, Udine: Mimesis, 2011. From a different point of view, see the earlier: Alessandro Bertante, *Contro il'68. La generazione infinita*, Milan: Agenzia X, 2007, whose subtitle captures the 'we still want everything and always will' of the leaders of the'68 generation still in positions of power.

6. Nanni Balestrini, *We Want Everything: A Novel*, trans. Matt Holden, London: Verso, 2022.

7. Paradoxes in the modern dispute over whether actors or spectators have the correct interpretation of events were first raised by Kant in his writings on the French Revolution (e.g., *The Conflict of Faculties*, trans. Mary J. Gregor, Lincoln, NE: University of Nebraska Press, 1992), admirably annotated by Hannah Arendt in her *Lectures on Kant's Political Philosophy*, (ed. Ronald Beiner, Brighton: Harvester, 1982). Neither unscathed, nor resolved in the providentialism of Hegelian idealism (history does what it has to do, and the sacrifice of individuals is the currency of the return of the spirit to itself), the issue reemerges powerfully in the classics of nineteenth-century historical-political reflection, from Marx's *The Eighteenth Brumaire Of Louis Bonaparte* to Tocqueville's *The Old Regime and the Revolution*, where men do make their own history, but often achieve the opposite of what they set out to do. It's almost too cruel to dwell on how the twentieth century has done its upmost to confirm this assumption.

8. Cited in Annette Wieviorka, *The Era of the Witness*, trans. Jared Stark, Ithaca, NY: Cornell University Press, 2006, 102–3. Alongside Wieviorka's book, for reasons evident from its title, see also:

Esther Benbassa, *Suffering as Identity: The Jewish Paradigm*, trans. G. M. Goshgarian, London: Verso, 2010.

9. Jean Améry, *At the Mind's Limits*, trans. Sidney Rosenfeld and Stella P. Rosenfeld, Bloomington & Indianapolis: Indiana University Press, 2009, 93.

10. Gideon Hausner, *Justice in Jerusalem*, New York: Harper & Row, 1966, 323.

11. Hausner, *Justice in Jerusalem*, 292.

12. On the debate about the uniqueness and comparability of the Shoah with other genocides, see the very balanced: Valentina Pisanty, *Abusi di memoria. Negare, banalizzare, sacralizzare la Shoah*, Milan: Bruno Mondadori, 2012.

13. Idith Zertal, *Israel's Holocaust and the Politics of Nationhood*, trans. Chaya Galai, Cambridge: Cambridge University Press, 2005.

14. Zertal, *Israel's Holocaust*, 169.

15. The bibliography on post-Vietnam cinematography is vast. Of note, in Italian, are: S. Ghislotti e S. Rosso, ed., *Vietnam e ritorno. La 'guerra sporca' nel cinema, nella narrativa, nel teatro, nella musica e nella cultura bellica degli Stati Uniti*, Milan: Marcos y Marcos, 1996. See also Stefano Rosso's excellent *Musi gialli e berretti verdi. Narrazioni Usa sulla guerra del Vietnam*, Bergamo: Sestante, 2003.

16. Allen Ginsberg, 'Howl', *Collected Poems, 1947–1985*, London: Penguin Books, 1995, 126.

17. Marco Saggioro has written a comprehensive dissertation on the theme of the victim in Pasolini's work, *La vittima nel cinema e nei film di Pier Paolo Pasolini*, which can be read at www.pasolini.net, which has provided many insights.

18. Cited in Tommaso Subini, *Pier Paolo Pasolini: La ricotta*, Turin: Lindau, 2009, 25. On the conflictual relationship between Fortini and Pasolini, see: Luca Lenzini, *Un'antica promessa: Studi su Fortini*, Macerata: Quodlibet, 2013.

19. Pier Paolo Pasolini, ed. and trans. Stephen Sartarelli, *The Selected Poetry of Pier Paolo Pasolini: A Bilingual Edition*, Chicago: University of Chicago Press, 17, translation expanded.

20. *Selected Poetry of Pier Paolo Pasolini*, 113.

21. Pier Paolo Pasolini, *Tutte le poesie*, vol. 1 & 2, ed. Walter Siti, Milan: Mondadori, 2009, 1155.

22. *Selected Poetry of Pier Paolo Pasolini*, 357.

23. *Selected Poetry of Pier Paolo Pasolini*, 175.

24. For these astute readings of Pasolini's work, see Alfonso Berardinelli, *Tra il libro e la vita*, Turin: Bollati Boringhieri, 1990, and Gianfanco Contini, *Ultimi esercizi ed elzeviri (1968–1987)*, Turin: Einaudi, 1988.

25. Pier Paolo Pasolini, *Saggi sulla politica e sulla società*, ed. Walter Siti and Silvia De Laude, Milan: Mondadori, 1999, 706–707.

26. Walter Siti, 'Elsa Morante nell'opera di Pier Paolo Pasolini', in: *Studi novecenteschi*, 47–48,1994.

27. Elsa Morante, *History*, trans. William Weaver, New York: Random House, 1984, 479.

28. Morante, *History*, 546.

29. Morante, *History*, 512.

30. Primo Levi, *The Drowned and the Saved*, trans. Raymond Rosenthal, New York: Random House, 1989, 57–58.

31. A massacre in which a bomb placed on a train by neo-fascists claimed 12 lives and wounded 48.

32. *L'amata. Lettere di e a Elsa Morante*, ed. D. Morante, Turin: Einaudi, 2012, 581.

33. Franco 'Bifo' Berardi, *Dell'innocenza: Interpretazione del'77*, Bologna: Agalev, 1987. On the contradictory nexus of innocence and memory in recollections of the 1970s, helpful has also been Andrea Hajek, 'Tracce urbane di un conflitto permanente. La memoria pubblica dei fatti di marzo'77 a Bologna', in *Etnografia e ricerca qualitativa*, 3, 2010.

34. Nolte's essay, 'The Past That Will Not Pass', may be found in *Forever in The Shadow of Hitler?* ed. Ernst Piper, Atlantic Highlands: Humanities Press, 1993, 18–23, 22. On the *Historikerstreit*, see also: Gian Enrico Rusconi, *Germania: un passato che non passa*, Turin: Einaudi, 1987.

35. A lively examination of the contemporary obsession with plagiarism may be found in Marie Darrieussecq, *Rapport de police: accusations de plagiat et autres modes de surveillance de la fiction*, Paris: P.O.L., 2014.

36. See: Catharine A. Mackinnon, *Only Words*, Cambridge, MA: Harvard University Press, 1993; Nadine Strossen, *Defending Pornography*, New York: NYU Press, 2000; Judith Butler, *Excitable Speech: A Politics of the Performative*, London: Routledge, 1997. A

fine essay by Emiliana Galiani, 'La pornografia come atto linguis-
tico: dimensione illocutoria e perlocutoria del performativo', in
Esercizi filosofici, 6, 2011, frames the terms and theoretical background of the debate clearly.

37. Ian Buruma, *Murder in Amsterdam: The Death of Theo Van Gogh
and the Limits of Tolerance*, London: Penguin, 2006.

Chapter Three

Abstract The chapter differentiates critique and satire: where the former requires empathy, the latter often ends up punching down rather than up. The mythology of the victim takes strength away from the weakest and places it in powerful hands, and the critic's task is to reshuffle the cards. The chapter argues that victimhood provides a fixed identity, reducing individuals to their trauma while undermining their agency. Drawing on Arendt, it shows how the idea of inalienable rights has been distortedly applied to victimhood, promoting a static view of the self, where identity is all about ownership rather than action. Thirty years of individualistic ideology have lent the concept of identity the popularity it now enjoys, in academia too. The chapter ends by interrogating the centrality of victim narratives in contemporary conspiracy theories and suggesting the centring of different myths to take the place of narratives of victimhood.

Keywords Victimhood · Satire · Identity · Innocence · Storytelling · Conspiracy theories · Myths

The critic interprets symptoms: not a doctor diagnosing, nor a surgeon amputating, but a guinea pig reflecting on experiments carried out on themselves. Critique without empathy may be perceptive but will always remain sterile; though rhetorically brilliant, that's what keeps pamphlets such as Robert Hughes' *The Culture of Complaint*, Pascal Bruckner's *The Tyranny of Guilt* or Norman Finkelstein's *The Holocaust Industry* from capturing the truth and depth of their subject matter. But the same may be said of a Swiftian satire like *My Holocaust* by Tova Reich, former wife of the director of the Holocaust Memorial Museum in Washington, DC. In the novel, Holocaust survivor Maurice Messer and his son and business partner run a methodical operation commercially exploiting the Jewish tragedy (organising heritage trips, long-distance adoptions, producing souvenirs and merchandise). On one such trip to Auschwitz, they run into a kind of assorted rainbow coalition that claims the right for all— not just the lucky ones (!)—to have a Holocaust of their own. Besides the Roma, Palestinian and Tibetan Holocausts, this includes: 'the ferret holocaust, the mad cow holocaust, the experimental and research animals holocaust, the right-to-bear-arms holocaust, the Confederate flag holocaust, the Falun Gong holocaust, the witches and Wiccans holocaust, the aliens and extraterrestrials holocaust, and so on and so forth'.[1]

The *reductio ad absurdum* we find in *My Holocaust* is perhaps the inevitable reversal of the *reductio ad Hitlerum* mentioned above. But reversing alone leaves us in the domain of what's been reversed. Far more liberating in scope are works like Philip Roth's American Trilogy (*American Pastoral, I Married a Communist, The Human Stain*) or Art Spiegelman's *Maus*, which depict the hell that's unleashed when the machine is set in motion that turns victims into guiltless perpetrators by virtue of their victimhood (Art's father, for example, once a deportee with a harrowing backstory, is now a schemer, stingy through and through, racist, misogynistic and manipulative even when his tears are sincere—with devastating effects on his son).

It's to these examples that we must turn. Satire tramples by trade is one-sided by vocation, but remains ambiguous, always running the risk of shifting from deriding the powerful to mocking the humble (as proven by the Medieval genre of the *satira del villano*, the satire of the peasant). A remnant of ancient cannibalism survives in the satirist, Walter Benjamin wrote of Karl Kraus, consuming adversaries to inherit their strength.[2] Sarcasm is suited only to reach the outermost circle of our target: the powerful who play the victims, the opportunists profiting from it. It loses all its bite when the cases become more ambiguous. Critique is the work that reason does for duty, compassion, concern for the common lot— the *pietas* at the root of pity. Victim mythology takes power away from the weakest and concentrates it in the wrong hands. Critiquing it means reshuffling the cards.

WHAT MORE DO YOU NEED?

It's only worth dwelling on the victimhood of the powerful, because it hegemonises the resentment of their subordinates. The process works through an identification analogous but inverse to that described by Freud in *Group Psychology and the Analysis of the Ego* (where the transference is propelled by the leader's potency, not his suffering). Such contagion has characterised, for example, all attempts at secession (successful or not) over the past two decades, in the Balkans, Italy or the Caucasus, where it's the elites who rebel—the rich who want to be free of the poor and shed the burden of paying taxes, which they see as an intolerable imposition. The winners' victimising rancour is one of the most singular phenomena of our times, collected in countless oral and written documents, even elevated to self-standing editorial subgenre: railing against 'the left' or against 'intellectuals' (the quotation marks are necessary, and the list could be much longer), with an obsessive litany worthy of an exorcist's ritual. If they're right, if history, as they like to say, has proven them right, why not just take it easy? What are they afraid of? Isn't resentment the servant's passion? Why choose resentment as the means of legitimising their rule? Why not just point to themselves as illustrious models? What are they lacking? What more do they need?

But lack is precisely the crux of our argument. The victim, the person who has had something taken away from them (rights, recognition, resources, life), is the symbol of choice for a defect of praxis, legitimacy, truth. Symbol and, at the same time, surrogate, filler or antidote. Satire is vain here—for if all satire is reversal, reversing a reversal is a zero-sum game. The victim is a reversed good. There's nothing good (in the double meaning of desirable and just) about the condition of victimhood, especially in an ethics that can give itself a name and a norm only by mythologising it. Getting to the bottom of the lack victimhood fills means explaining its capacity for cognitive distortion,[3] in George Lakoff's terms, and thereby hopefully breaking free of it. What are the promises and prohibitions of an imaginary that's made passivity its magnetic north?

INALIENABLE

First, victimhood promises identity. The victim *is* something, has an origin and papers, is constituted by an event, is ascertainable and indisputable. Victimhood interpellates, with certainty and authority. What am I? A victim, and that can never be denied or taken away from me. Victimhood frames being in terms of having, reduces the subject to a bearer of property (rather than an actor), and asks them to remain, painfully but proudly, what they are. It demands no transformation, renunciation or sacrifice. The sacrifice has already happened, and no more is needed: we've already pulled our weight, now we're entitled to rest in ourselves. This is a desirable goal for those who believe change is impossible, especially when the powerful have everything to gain from this scepticism, which leaves things as they are—that is, in their hands. Victimhood castrates agency, in the word's multiple meanings. A genuine victim is such because they are powerless. That's how the imaginary victim justifies their powerlessness; or, if they can't claim to be powerless, their desire to remain what they are by inalienable property rights.

Inalienable—in other words: spectral, phantasmal, insubstantial. For inalienable rights don't exist in nature, they're enjoyed only by the citizens of the *polis*, as Hannah Arendt, in *The Origins of Totalitarianism*, understood before anyone else. Nothing is more abstract than human rights, which tellingly become a problem only when political rights are denied, because it's the latter that ground the former, not the other way around.[4] But what is insubstantial is also plastic and adaptable, exempt from verification, endlessly reproducible even as contexts change, such that it undermines the already porous barrier between real and imagined victimisation. Doesn't psychoanalysis tell us that our ego—the very thing we take the most pride in, what we believe to be our most cherished, most definite and authentic possession—is in fact shaped by mirroring and projection? (And rivalry and aversion—think of the mirror phase: who's that over there behaving like me?) That it is, in a word, as imaginary as it gets?

Only thirty years of unchallenged cult of the individual could give the concept of identity the prominence it enjoys today, where it's even managed to breach the citadel of supposedly critical thought. Such are the miracles of hegemony. One need only observe the flourishing in English and American academia of departments devoted to stigmatised social groups: Women studies, Black studies, Gay studies, Queer studies, and, of course, Holocaust studies (outgrowth and origin of Memory studies and Trauma studies), and many others. Everyone is in search of an identity. An identity not thought of naturalistically, as an essential fact (the horror! That would violate the first commandment of postmodern episteme)—if anything, as performative, hybrid, changeable, a linguistic construct, a cultural negotiation. In any case, still something (if words have any meaning) derived from *idem*, the Latin pronoun denoting the permanence of the same. The quintessentially modern imperative, 'You must change your life', commanded to Rilke by the archaic torso of Apollo, dedicatee of his well-known poem, has been replaced by a less binding, but no less exigent, 'You must find yourself, you must *be* yourself'. Victims find this easier to do, and genuine victims are unfortunately compelled to. And it's easier still for those who, without much theoretical sophistication, promise a simple return to roots, values and traditions: How else to understand the expansion of radical Islamism after the disillusions of post-colonial independence? To be surprised such forces have roundly defeated the well-meaning proponents of performative identity requires a naiveté that it's hard to pity.

Victim mythology is a response to what's been termed the end of the 'grand narratives' of emancipation—of the possibility, in other words, of the 'nothing' (those who cannot, those who don't know, those who must not) becoming 'everything', as the Abbé Sieyès said of the Third Estate at the beginning of the French Revolution. A response that expects and embeds defeat. The narratives that literally shattered the Hegelian dialectic of lord and bondsman—I am the bondsman and *for that very reason* don't fear death—have been replaced by the anxiety of recognition driving narratives of identity. 'What is to be done?', the question that has dominated modern politics, has given way to the querulous 'Who am I?'. And, in a sense, answering 'A victim' isn't entirely incorrect. Those who are limited only to asking who they are, and not what they can do with themselves and their relationships with others, are, by definition, victims.

As well as being unfaithful to history, victimary ideology is also unfaithful to nature, we might say, to our shared heritage as a species. To understand this we must exercise what Foucault called an 'ontology of the present'—namely, the seemingly paradoxical intersection of two logically distinct planes: on one side, something that *always is*, an unvarying dimension that determines being since it's part of humanity's biological makeup; on the other, the appearance of an external manifestation that becomes visible *only now*, issuing from what's currently happening.

For example, one of humanity's insurmountable horizons is the condition of vulnerability, exposure and dependence described above. But only in recent times has this condition been elevated to unsound grounding of identity, when it's clear that our species has adapted successfully by reacting against it, rather than submitting to it.

Indeed, a primary characteristic of the human animal—lacking an environment shaped by instincts, as is the case with other species—is a twofold constraint: to be open to the radical contingency of a world in which everything can become meaningful, while at the same time delimiting that contingency by establishing a network of symbols that circumscribe it: culture. This isn't because man lives beyond nature, as twentieth-century philosophical anthropology (Gehlen, Plessner, Heidegger) would argue. Rather, his weak instinctual equipment and congenital inability to distinguish between the internal and external, between signal (what's pertinent to survival) and noise (what isn't), are undoubtedly the result of a complex evolutionary process that's anything but preternatural. But forging a habitable environment in a boundless world is only possible for a plastic, versatile animal; to adapt, man must continually transform himself and the external reality he shapes, including within his remit of action that same openness to boundless contingency he sets out to exorcise. Hallmark of our nature is not just the preservation of order, but also its continual subversion. Naturally artificial, man is naturally revolutionary. Change is his hypseity.[5] Identity is the opposite of revolution.

Never before, however, has mankind lived through such radically counter-revolutionary times. Proof of this is that reversing the idea of revolution gives us a precise and reliable cartography of our present. It matches, point for point, if read in reverse. Revolution is what's missing, and its lack constitutes us, if we think of it not as concrete fact (reform, revolt, insurrection, seizing of power, etc.) but as a generic signifier, a modalizer that indicates and implicates a subject position, one anyone can hold. It stands in for everything it's natural to want to be: autonomous, aware, free from fear, not because we're allowed to but because we want to, not because of who we are but because of what we do. But it's also the opposite of what hegemony enjoins us to be today: submissive, afraid, in need of protection, yearning only to be governed—well, ideally, but if not it's all the same. 'Decisions', Lyotard writes on postmodernism, 'do not have to respect individuals' aspirations: the aspirations have to aspire to the decisions, or at least to their effects'.[6]

Revolution is the other name for modernity: subjecthood, responsibility, the capacity to make choices, even tragic ones, and a conception of other people not only as threat or constraint but as multipliers of power, creativity, imagination and pleasure. And if the word postmodern has any meaning at all, it's to be found in the specular inversion of these terms: identity, passivity, deresponsibilisation, seeing others as rivals, competitors and a source of resentment. On one side, a conception of happiness as something constitutively public, common, indivisible but shareable; on the other, the private happiness of the narrow escape, the larger piece of the pie, of envy projected onto others. On one side, critique; on the other, consensus. How, otherwise, can we explain the fanatical zeal with which apologists of the present rage against a corpse? Concretely, who fears a revolution anymore? Yet all we're asked to commit to memory is the warning that revolution produces victims. Which is true. And there's not much point retorting: counterrevolutions do too. Unless we clarify the key difference: taking upon itself the tragedy and 'absolute sinfulness' of humanity abandoned by the gods (to borrow Lukacs' well-known phrase), revolution produces contingent victims and would avoid them if it could, whereas counterrevolution produces eternal victims, better still if satisfied in their victimhood.

INNOCENCE

Second, as noted above, victimhood guarantees innocence. The pervasive need for innocence today is at once self-evident and a theological mystery. This isn't so much about the legitimate aspiration to do no harm, but the impossible desire to be declared incapable of doing so. With genuine victims, this de facto incapacity becomes *de jure*: if the victim could have defended themselves, they would not have become victims. But who envies such a status? Which failings does it speak to? Victimary mythology is the reaction to a praxis constitutively experienced as guilt. Hence the various strategies of expulsion, denial and projection, a prime example of which is the wholescale condemnation of the twentieth century, the guilty century, when for the first time praxis was considered a right, indeed a universal duty.

Analogous impetuses underpin our fascination with crime novels, conspiracies and serial killers, where the only (real) action possible is, by definition, criminal. 'There is no room / For guiltless action, 'tis only

given / To either inflict wrongs or suffer them',[7] was the bitter conclu-
sion reached by Prince Adelchis at the end of Alessandro Manzoni's play
of the same name. A position echoed by Renzo Tramaglino at the end
of Manzoni's novel *The Betrothed*, where the 'moral of the story' is that
'trouble often comes calling when it's been invited in. Not even the most
cautious and innocent behavior can keep it away. And when trouble does
come calling, rightly or wrongly, faith in God softens the blow'.[8] These
lines speak to Manzoni's openly conservative and tacitly tragic vision of
history, convinced there's no room for action that unites or divides man,
because only action taking place on the vertical, intangible plane of divine
grace is just and true. From *The Betrothed* to crime fiction is a long way to
go. But the distance is shortened if we keep in mind Siegfried Kracauer's
analysis of the commercial success of the detective novel as an expression
of secularised theological anxieties.[9] Desire for innocence and obsession
with guilt are two ways of saying the same thing.

This is increasingly true at a time when the concept of guilt has been
secularised, precisely, into that of debt. Or, as Nietzsche would say, it
has gone back to its origins: *Schuld*, in German, means both guilt and
debt. In *The Genealogy of Morality*, it's our internalisation of debt as a
lack or fault that generated ideas such as guilt, sin and bad conscience.[10]
We were first at fault towards our creditors, then our deified ancestors,
until the invention of the single god towards whom we're all indebted/
guilty—a condition concretised (not amnestied, as is commonly believed)
by Christianity, where it's the god who pays the price, since humanity
would never be able to. I'll do it, you won't manage alone. Your debt is
too big to pay off. Your guilt is original—it's your origin.

Debt and credit also underlie the mechanisms of capitalist accumula-
tion, Walter Benjamin argued in an early fragment entitled 'Capitalism
as Religion'.[11] This deep structure rises to the surface at times of radical
crisis, such as we're currently experiencing. Today, private and public debt
are the insuperable limits of our agency, with the creditor usurping the
throne formerly of the sovereign, as an incontestable authority vested with
the power to decree a state of emergency, whose word has the force of
law. Indebted and guilty ('we didn't force anyone to buy our derivatives',
one banker justified himself at the onset of the financial crisis), it's not
surprising that our age yearns for an escape, if not for the salvation that
praxis or politics are increasingly powerless even to promise. Persecuted
by reality, innocence takes refuge in the imaginary, and it's there that
it encounters the victim, the only one allowed to say: it's not my fault,

don't hold me to account. For a victim has no debts, only credits. An enviable condition, a paradoxical paradise, a narcotic masking the sinister implications of the irresponsible injunction to enjoy of the capitalist's discourse. *Resistance is Futile* is an aptly titled novel by Walter Siti, in which a formerly obese, antisocial outsider becomes a ruthless economic hitman in the pay of mafia finance. The victim draws innocence from the wellspring of evil.

My Story

Third, every victim has a story. Which endears them to a culture convinced that storytelling is everything. By now, writers have long cast off the suspicion of narrativity that characterised the great twentieth-century experiments. Find a good story is the first lesson of journalism school. But this precept has spread like wildfire to many other branches of the humanities: analytic or continental philosophy, from Arthur Danto to Paul Ricœur; neuroscience, of which Daniel Dennett is a leading light; historiography (Hayden White, Robert Darnton, Simon Schama); anthropology (Clifford Geertz, Marc Augé, James Clifford); psychology (Jerome Bruner); cultural studies (Homi K. Bhabha), and the list could go on. All agree that identity, both personal and collective, is the narrative each person tells about themselves. Identity itself is narrative. *Homo sapiens = homo narrans*. Every person is their story, and every nation too. And the same applies to products, companies and election campaigns.

From marketing to political communication, human resources to business strategy, leadership training to customer, employee and voter preferences, there's no section of society untouched by the need to be imagined, structured and experienced as a story, one which assigns clear roles and values and prescribes the goals and desires of its narrator.[12] We know full well the impact spin doctors have on our politics, how the Pentagon worked with Hollywood, how simulation games are used to train the military or rehabilitate from post-traumatic stress syndrome. Big business is reorganising under the sign of storytelling. Gone is the silence of the Fordist factory; labour relations are now dominated by narratives hijacked by management to direct aspirations, arouse fears, promote loyalty and neutralise conflicts. Strategies for industrial and financial expansion are planned as fictions, novels, movies, even fairy tales. Where logical reasoning is boring, mere calculation chilling and images alone discomforting (has it been doctored?), a good story is motivational, provides a fitting caption, establishes which emotional reactions it should elicit, and above all uses procedures fine-tuned in the laboratory of fiction to make it more 'realistic' (not in the sense that it cleaves closer to reality, but is verisimilar, coherent and shareable).

But this raises a problem. One need not have read Propp and Greimas to know that stories all look alike and can be classified according to a small number of recurring elements, varied and combined more or less adroitly, but which remain recognisable. Such stereotypy may be reassuring (children wisely have no problem asking to be told the same story over and over again), but it may also generate anguish, ontological disquiet, dere-alisation anxiety: am I really me, or just an archetype who answers to my name? Why should anyone listen to me if my story's already been told a thousand times? The more authentic one aspires to be, the more one ends up repeating oneself. The victim escapes this stricture: no one will ever accuse them of playing to stereotypes, for fear of being accused, in turn, of lacking empathy. No one will ever dismiss the victim's as 'the same old story'. No one will ever ask them to explain the 'how'—it's the 'what', the content, that matters. The victim's story is always convincing, marshalling attention, disciplining its reception, disqualifying the distinction between the good and the less so. This emotional blackmail is, in the best of cases, blameless; in the worst, contemptible; for the most part ambiguous. In all cases it's inescapable—just try it to believe it. The choice is between listening sympathetically or facing guilt and universal disapproval.

But the bond between victimhood and storytelling runs deeper. Story-telling is a device that tends towards simplification, totalisation and closure. Working under the logic of identity and consistency, of stitching together the irregular and homogenising the uneven, it proceeds by selec-tion, combination and exclusion of possibilities, until only one remains: the resolution or ending, whether happy or tragic. What's excluded from the story is obliterated, including what we don't remember, don't want to or cannot say, perhaps what others might have to say about us. Left to their own devices, stories are proprietary and totalitarian by nature. It's not for nothing that humans also have other forms of thought and communication: calculation, argumentation, analogy, dialogue, discourse in its broadest sense. Where stories bring together to separate—*my* story, *our* story, which doesn't belong to you—discourse divides to interre-late. Voices remain distinct and possibilities remain open. Critique isn't just confrontation, but mutual accretion, precisely what the condition of victimhood exempts us from. Which doesn't lead to the absurd conclu-sion that all storytelling is victimary or should be—although Don DeLillo did once voice a similar suspicion:

> Plots carry their own logic. There is a tendency of plots to move toward death. [...] A plot in fiction... is the way we localize the force of the death outside the book, play it off, contain it.[13]

There certainly is, in any case, an elective morphological affinity between victim narratives and narratives that refuse to incorporate elements of contradiction, complexity, ambiguity or confusion. Clarity, linearity, unambiguousness, accounts that add up: these are the ingredi-ents of winning stories. And with their axiology devoid of nuance, of light and shade, victim stories are the most successful of all. When all stories are equal, some stories are more equal than others.

Truth Equals Death

Finally, victims guarantee truth. They are, by definition, right. They need not question themselves. They need not examine or interpret anything. They're untroubled by the scruples with which more than a century of hermeneutics of suspicion has scrutinised the disturbing nexus of truth and power. That truth is what power decides is true doesn't concern them, for the victim is true when bereft of power, and wouldn't be a victim if it weren't so. Pontius Pilate's unsettling question, 'What is truth?', is his dubious privilege, and Christ chose rightly not to answer it, implying: it's right in front of you. Truth is undisputable only for victims of untruth. Truth may be doubtful, but we know untruth when we're subjected to it. Truth is subject to interpretation, whereas untruth can be proven.

This is a supremely desirable condition in an age suspended between a generalised scepticism and an uncritical desire to believe what we're told, delegate our responsibilities and rely nihilistically on those who tell us what to do. The victim is well aware of the truth of the person telling them what to do, and thus requires no hypocrisy, no turning of blind eyes. Girard rightly points out that even the most thorough nihilists decon-struct everything except the innocence of the victim. When weak thought was in vogue in Italy, it brought an outpouring of ethical prescriptions on terms such as care, attentiveness and protection (neglected, for Gianni

Vattimo and others, by so-called 'strong thought', too busy affirming itself to be concerned with suffering singularity).

All true, but not the whole story. Indeed, a sinister and inevitable consequence is, as we've seen, the proliferation of alleged, potential, would-be and sometimes patently false victims. One can't escape from the truth-power cycle quite so easily. If truth lies only in the victim, those who seek to lend their words a chrism of truth will always be tempted to pass themselves off as such. The lack of a truth and an idea of good that can be pointed to as a positive, rather than negative, example makes ours a time of paralysis in terms of a praxis that aspires to be anything more than simply adaptive. Things aren't as you say they are: this is only half the work of critique. The other half is just as necessary: this is how they really are. That the suffering endured is our sole proof of injustice is the belated gratification of those who've abandoned all hope of winning. This was not how the Enlightenment, Marxism and feminism worked, to name but three examples; nor, unfortunately, do religious fundamentalisms. A 'no' without even the possibility of a 'yes' is a consolation prize not even worth collecting.

A clear example comes in *Romanzo di una strage* [*Piazza Fontana: The Italian Conspiracy*], Marco Tullio Giordana's film about the Piazza Fontana bombing of 1969, with its naive (or cunning; at any rate irritating) dichotomy between the good guys, i.e., those who died (Pinelli the anarchist, Commissioner Calabresi, Aldo Moro), and the bad guys, i.e., those who organised and then covered up the bombing.[14] It's the bad guys who make history, while everyone else endures it. Good has no place in the story. But the counterweight of this tragic backdrop is an anti-tragic ethics, clear in the director's decision to deprive the characters of the possibility of participating in an evil that the film's axiological system identifies with action—that is, with politics, a politics mostly reduced to *ius neci*, the sovereign right to kill. (This despite the fact that Pinelli belongs to an anarchist movement that by no means repudiates violence, Commissioner Calabresi carries the sword as representative of the institutions that hold the monopoly of legitimate force, and former Prime Minister Moro is a man intimately acquainted with state secrets.) That even the good guys might be in conflict with each other, or have values that are complex and perhaps impossible to synthesise, is a thought that must never cross the viewer's mind. The only value to be proud of here is powerlessness.

In one of the film's final sequences, Calabresi is alone in his office at night. The camera frames him from three sides (he's a multifaceted character, clearly, with a complex inner life), then he turns and looks into the camera. On the other side is Pinelli, who looks up, flashing a sad smile. The two respected each other in life, and now they both know the truth, which has come too late, at death's door—a door Pinelli has already passed through and Calabresi is about to. The truth can be uttered only when it's useless. Indeed, *Romanzo di una strage* is symptomatic, rather than illustrative, of a relationship between awareness and history that's been shorn of all consequence; pity is the only work left for us to do. If truth is in the eye of the victim, truth equals death. A very clear warning to anyone who might want to seek out today's truth. We've all seen how the story ends. This is a morality of surrender, which the victim's iconostasis compensates with a dignity it doesn't deserve.

This is accompanied, however, by a complicity not easily shed. It's difficult to measure up to a nihilism that hasn't rained down from the heavens, but is, as Vico reminds us, the product of the world as we have made it. The human world has no transcendent truth with which to refute a statement, reject a doctrine or oppose a policy; and it's understandable, albeit sad, that we turn to the victim as our final appeal, the Supreme Court of history. Understandable, but paralysing. It's both necessary and difficult to instead accept that there are only practices to be pitted against practices, interests against interests, values against values: truth against truth—a term that perhaps, as Alain Badiou has long maintained, should be used in the plural, without thereby watering it down into the pluralism of compatibility at all costs and mutual accreditation as a higher law. Truths may be in conflict, and there is no such thing as a general ethics because there is no such thing as a universal subject to act as its spokesperson, no incorporeal shadow which the victim gives substance to with their suffering body. Ethics is the 'labour', Badiou writes, 'that brings *some* truths into the world'.[15] A labour in which one can yield— but certainly not as victims—whereas there's nothing more nihilistic than an ethics based solely on having been harmed, whether in reality or potentially. Built on the constant threat of annihilation, the mythology of victimhood becomes a religion of death.

Polyphemus

Let's go over the charges one last time. Prosopopoeia of the victim strengthens the powerful and weakens the subaltern. It hollows out agency. It perpetuates pain. It fosters resentment. It enshrines the imaginary. It fuels rigid and often fictitious identities. It nails us to the past and mortgages the future. It discourages transformation. It privatises history. It confuses freedom with irresponsibility. It glorifies powerlessness or cloaks it in usurped power. In cahoots with death, it makes a show of mourning life. It covers up the emptiness underlying all universal ethics. It eliminates—indeed rejects—conflict, and cries outrage at contradiction. It prevents us from understanding the real lack we feel, which is a deficiency of praxis, politics and common action.

We've seen these charges resurface cyclically in very different situations and circumstances. There's enough evidence here for a conviction without appeal. We're not in a court of law, however, and critique that seeks only to reach a judgement—especially a condemnation—wastes its trump card. No dialectical sleight of hand can magically turn negative into positive. Underlying the prestige the victim currently enjoys is the wrong answer to a right question; a latent truth waiting to be teased out; a signpost that's been turned upside down or reversed. Questioning the victim in this light is the highest form of compassion possible. It's not just a matter of describing phenomena but of rescuing them—this was the Platonic school maxim Walter Benjamin borrowed to read German Baroque's tragic drama as an allegory of his time—by identifying not only their underlying structure, but the potential forces that determine them. Potential implies the possibility of things being different, that this 'just so' could also not be 'just so'. Potential is agency's best translation.

Indeed, the ways of the victim inevitably lead us back to (denied) agency. In rejecting agency—in exchange for compensation, exemptions, privileges and false consciousness—victimary mythology continually points to its presence in others: someone else, not me, is responsible. Neither blind, inscrutable fate; nor the whim of gods or heavens; nor the innocence of becoming; nor the ownerless algorithms of finance, but identifiable historical subjects, accountable by name and surname, class and condition, ideology and behaviour. If things are as they are, it's because someone has done something—and this attests to the fact that something can indeed be done. It all depends on what and especially who, on which side one wants to be on. The victim doesn't accept justifications on behalf of higher interests (God's will, reason of state, happiness of the people, race supremacy, classless society, needs of production, EU imposi-tions…), as they cannot disregard the particularities of their own story. In this lies their weakness but also their moment of truth: by denying their responsibility and magnifying that of others, it's still real responsibility that's at stake.

Something similar characterises another contemporary mythology, closely related to the victim's—that of conspiracy theories, of a universal, ubiquitous conspiracism, as humiliating counterweight to the comman-deering of effective action in the sphere of (supposed) systemic rationality. The most widespread and shallow explanation goes like this: society and history are complex; long dead are the philosophies and ideolo-gies promising subjects the possibility of rationalising the nexus between causes and effects, means and ends, and thus determining the course of events; that possibility has now been taken over by the system; and individual and collective initiative is little more than a bit player, a contin-gency deprived of necessity. Unable to stand it, the weakest and clueless rack their brains for whose fault it could be, to which the obsession with conspiracy provides an easy but deceptive answer. Those who, like Polyphemus, only ask 'Who's doing me wrong?' can only be mocked or pitied, like the Cyclopes did with Polyphemus: no one's doing you wrong, let us sleep.

But for all his wrongs, Polyphemus was right about something. Someone had, after all, put his eye out. The idea persists, in the conspir-acist's distorted rationality, that history is made by men and women, not impersonal and unaccountable agencies—a conception that's still grounded in modernity. A modernity that is upturned, blinded and denied, perhaps, as with deresponsibilising victimhood, but which still has the strength to express its reasons and needs, albeit through the estranged language of the symptom. Conspiracy fiends and victim leaders reveal what they conceal, affirm what they deny, stare at what they can't see: in their surrender is a residue of struggle, in their renunciation a trace of desire, in their misplaced pride the sign of a possible, legitimate pride. Read in reverse, their fallacy is the language of truth.

When not in blatant bad faith, the prosopopoeia of the victim is a protest (powerless and dangerous, if left to its own devices) against the breakdown of the public sphere experienced by citizens in post-democratic societies. Even in bad faith, it still taps into the same reservoir of passions. The strength of the deceivers draws parasitically on the strength of the deceived. Returning that strength to those who've been dispossessed of it is what critique of the victim sets out to do. This is what happened, for example, when the labour movement went from the 'philosophy of misery' (in Marx's phrase) to the critical pride of those who, knowing they are at the forefront of social production, demand the right to lead it—the right to act, in other words, and not simply exist through suffering. '*Debout les damnés de la terre*': the hymn of the international workers' movement addresses the 'wretched of the earth', but urges them to 'arise'.

The first step is to begin to see ourselves (once again) as interested parties, rather than representatives of the spectral universality promised by a victimary ethics. Victimhood demands a unanimous response, but a unanimous response is a false one, which obscures the real fault lines of division, injustice and inequality that characterise power relations. Politics and conflict are synonyms. As Jacques Rancière reminds us, politics is when there are at least two ideas about how to divide up the world. It's 'police', not politics, when there's only one—in the eighteenth-century meaning of policy, business as usual, the well-oiled machinery of the status quo. That the victim clearly lubricates this machine is a brazen paradox, when they should be a stumbling block, a scandal, a breakpoint in its operation. Victim mythology is a subalternity that perpetuates domination. It would be excessively optimistic, belying a naive idea of power, to believe they'll disappear together someday. But this is the order of the day, and each day has enough trouble of its own.

DIFFERENT MYTHS?

We'll conclude not with a recipe or prescription, but with a doubt. Critique has taken us this far. The onus then moves to praxis, and praxis isn't determined theoretically, nor devised alone. Not because there's an unbridgeable gap between the two—critique is theory inherent in praxis, if theory doesn't mean projecting a grid of stable forms onto mutable phenomena, but rather taking a step backwards to the point where the phenomena take shape. Critique is engendered in the crisis of what Wittgenstein called 'a form of life',[16] that is, a set of norms that have become a *habitus*. When a norm ceases to apply because it allows for too many discordant applications (in our case: the untenable ethical polysemy of the victim), we're back in a realm where rules show they are contingent, and can thus be rediscussed, transformed or abrogated.

But that critique alone is enough to achieve this, there's the rub. Many have suggested, with varying degrees of cautiousness, that we also need new myths, which are not subaltern in nature. This was argued, with some uneasiness, by Furio Jesi in *Spartakus: The Symbology of Revolt*, written in the wake of 1968. It's repeated today, with a refreshing optimism that it'd be nice to wholly underwrite, by Yves Citton in *Mythocracy: How Stories Shape Our Worlds*.[17] It's pondered articulately and thoughtfully by the writers who gather in the Wu Ming collective.

It is possible. Desirable too? It's certainly dangerous, as countless examples prove. Many years ago, and in very different contexts, even Louis Althusser—an advocate of the idea that history is a process without subject and telos governed only by the variable geometry of the nexus between productive forces and relations of production—recognised that human praxis can't exist in the absence of ideology, if by ideology we mean the necessary imaginative awareness of the position the individual holds in reality. But what truth can be built on imagination? And is there not in the very structure of myths an inertial tendency to pose as a justification, aetiology, even theodicy of power? The matter deserves further investigation. Clearly, we're just getting started.

NOTES

1. Tova Reich, *My Holocaust*, New York: Harper Collins, 2007, 284.
2. Walter Benjamin, 'Karl Kraus', trans. Edmund Jephcott, *Walter Benjamin Selected Writings Volume 2, 1927–1934*, ed. Michael Jennings, Howard Eiland and Gary Smith, Cambridge, MA: Belknap Press/Harvard University Press, 1999, 433–458.
3. See George Lakoff, *The Political Mind*, New York: Viking, 2008.
4. Hannah Arendt, *The Origins of Totalitarianism*, Cleveland, OH: Meridian, 1962. See also: Jacques Rancière, *Dissensus: On Politics and Aesthetics*, ed. and trans. Steve Corcoran, London: Continuum, 2010, and Slavoj Zizek, 'Against Human Rights', *New Left Review*, 34, July–August 2005.
5. See, on this: Massimo De Carolis, *The Anthropological Paradox*, trans. Richard Bates, London: Routledge, 2018, and Paolo Virno, *E così via, all'infinito. Logica e antropologia*, Turin: Bollati Boringhieri, 2010.
6. Jean-François Lyotard, *The Postmodern Condition: A Report on Knowledge*, Minneapolis: University of Minnesota Press, 1985, 62.

Lyotard's bitter observation on the reversal of the nexus between aspiration and decision is clearly derived from Niklas Luhmann's systems theory.

7. Alessandro Manzoni, *The Count of Carmagnola and Adelchis*, ed. and trans. Federica Brunori Deigan, Baltimore and London: The Johns Hopkins University Press, 2004, 306.

8. Alessandro Manzoni, *The Betrothed*, trans. Michael Moore, New York: Random House, 2024, 648.

9. Siegfried Kracauer, *Schriften I*, Frankfurt: Suhrkamp, 1971, 103–204.

10. Friedrich Nietzsche, *On the Genealogy of Morality*, ed. Keith Ansell-Pearson, trans. Carol Diethe, Cambridge: Cambridge University Press, 2007.

11. Walter Benjamin, 'Capitalism as religion'. In: M. Bullock & M. W. Jennings (eds.), *Walter Benjamin Selected Writings: Vol. 1: 1913–1926*, Cambridge, MA: Belknap Press/Harvard University Press, 1996, 289–291. For a rigorous commentary, see Elettra Stimilli, *Debt and Guilt: A Political Philosophy*, trans. Stefania Porcelli, London and New York: Bloomsbury Academic, 2019, and Roberto Esposito, *Two: The Machine of Political Theology and the Place of Thought*, trans. Zakiya Hanafi, New York: Fordham University Press, 2015.

12. For a comprehensive and balanced review of storytelling's place in theory and contemporary culture, see: Donata Meneghelli, *Storie proprio così. Il racconto nell'era della narratività totale*, Milan: Morellini, 2013. On the broader issue of the spread of literary vocabulary and techniques to other fields of knowledge, see the comprehensive: Remo Ceserani, *Convergenze. Gli strumenti letterari e le altre discipline*, Milan: Mondadori, 2010.

13. Don DeLillo, *Libra*, New York: Viking, 1988, 221.

14. For more on plots and coverups, death and ideology in contemporary Italy, through the prism of Giordana's film *Romanzo di una strage*—an improbable reconstruction of the Piazza Fontana massacre—see Daniele Giglioli, 'La favola di una strage', in *Meridiana*, 73–74, 2012.

15. Alain Badiou, *Ethics: An Essay on the Understanding of Evil*, trans. Peter Hallward, London: Verso, 2012, 28. For Badiou, the victim mythology underlying contemporary ethics is unable to generate 'truths in the plural'. The conception of truth as necessarily biased

(and not unanimous or shared), resulting from conflict rather than agreement, underlies the thought of Jacques Rancière, whose *Dissensus* is cited above.

16. Ludwig Wittgenstein, *Philosophical Investigations*, ed. G.E.M. Anscombe, New York: Wiley-Blackwell, 1953. This argument is developed from Paolo Virno, *Motto di spirito e azione innovativa. Per una logica del cambiamento*, Turin: Bollati Boringhieri, 2005.

17. The dangerous nexus between mythology and emancipatory political praxis has been explored by Yves Citton, *Mythocratie. Storytelling et imaginaire de gauche*, Paris: Éditions Amsterdam, 2010 (an English translation is forthcoming with Verso with the title *Mythocracy: How Stories Shape Our Worlds*), and Furio Jesi, *Spartakus: The Symbology of Revolt*, trans. Alberto Toscano, London and Calcutta: Seagull Books, 2024.

Correction to: Critique of the Victim

Correction to:
D. Giglioli, *Critique of the Victim,*
https://doi.org/10.1007/978-3-031-80132-7

The original version of this book was inadvertently published with an error in the country name in the copyright page initially, which has now been corrected. The book has been updated with the changes.

The updated version of this book can be found at
https://doi.org/10.1007/978-3-031-80132-7

C1

INDEX

The manufacturer's authorised representative in the EU is Springer
Nature Customer Service Centre GmbH, Europaplatz 3, 69115 Heidelberg,
Germany. If you have any concerns regarding our products, please
contact ProductSafety@springernature.com

Printed and bound by CPI Group (UK) Ltd, Croydon, CR0 4YY

29/04/2026

02099545-0003